THE BREATH OF LOVE

MICHEL QUOIST

THE
BREATH OF
LOVE

Translated by N. D. Smith

Crossroad • New York

1987

The Crossroad Publishing Company
370 Lexington Avenue, New York, N.Y. 10017

Originally published in France by
Les Editions Ouvrières, Paris, under
the title *Parle-moi d'amour*
© Michel Quoist 1985

Translation © Gill and Macmillan 1986

Printed in the United States of America

Library of Congress Cataloging in Publication Data

Quoist, Michel.
    The breath of love.

    Translation of: Parle-moi d'amour.
    Includes index.
    1. Love—Religious aspects—Christianity—Meditations.
I. Title
BV4639.Q6513   1987   241'.4   87-538
ISBN 0-8245-0852-1
ISBN 0-8245-0801-7 (pbk.)

Contents

THE BREATH OF LOVE

Introduction:
to my friends – my readers

The first thing that I want to say is: Please read the whole of this introduction!

If you do this, you will not have to look in the book itself for things that I did not want to put in it. You will also learn why I have made extensive use of a way of writing that I have not employed before. In fact, if you are familiar with my other books, you may be surprised by the literary form of this one, since it is quite different from that of my previous work.

Love has become a commonplace thing

It is common knowledge that love is devalued in the modern world. At the risk of generalising, it would not be wrong to say that many people no longer believe in love and especially in love between man and woman. Marriage? It is no longer necessary, they say. Faithfulness? Just not possible now. Living together? Essential. Love? That is just a physically pleasurable technique that can be learned, something that you have to succeed in.

Love is no longer a taboo subject. You can talk about it – luckily. Boys and girls are soon initiated into it. But what form does that initiation take? The emphasis is biological, structured and technical: How to 'make love' successfully and safely and so on.

But some young people are becoming tired of soulless instruction and disappointing experiences, while others, older perhaps, are glad to have been liberated from the prejudices and constraints of the past, but know that their adventures have not brought happinness.

Is love really intended to be something quite different? Some people are beginning to sense that it is and want to

1

discover it. In some countries — the United States, for example — faithfulness and even virginity before marriage are being rediscovered. New hopes are emerging. I think they are a sign of a new appeal to lead a life that would be in danger of dying if love were to die.

Love is a great mystery

We have to restore love to its true place in life and give it back in true dimension. Its true place is in the human heart and the heart of the history of the world. It is the power — the essential Energy — of life without which neither we nor the world can grow harmoniously and know happiness. Its true dimension is infinity. Love goes beyond love! It comes from elsewhere and goes elsewhere. Christians believe it comes from and goes to God, since God 'is' Love.

Man and wife and the home are at the centre of this great Adventure of love. It becomes flesh and makes life live. God himself who is Love — God-love — took on a human face and became flesh in order to give us life.

What is this book about?

It is not a scientific study of love. Nor does it provide useful hints about how to succeed in love. It is certainly not an exemplary 'love story'. No, it is a set of reflections and meditations about love. My aim in bringing these texts together is to help you to discover — or rediscover — the beauty and the greatness of love and also the demands that it makes.

These meditations are set within the framework of a story — that of a young man making regular visits to an older man. This 'Sage' guides his young disciple in his search for love and his discovery of it. The story is just an artificial prop or a human device used to introduce each meditation. The personalities of the two leading actors have been barely sketched in. Not even their faces have been described. The story framework has been deliberately left vague. I have also tried to go beyond individual circumstances. This is so that you have the freedom to enable you to find your own way in your search for your own heart, using my text as your guide.

2

Reality or unreality?

Why, then, have I chosen this way of writing? It would seem to be a long way from real life. It is because I wanted to put the poetry back into love, to give it back its depths by letting the reader sense its mystery.

We shall never fully succeed in producing love electronically in a programmed state from our computers. Scientific research will never make it reveal its ultimate secrets. The reality of love in all its dimensions will only be discovered in contemplation. Poetry may be one approach to it. (We should never think of poetry as unreal. It is a way of coming closer to the inner reality that goes beyond ordinary knowledge and can only be understood in symbols.)

The limits of this book

The Adventure of love embraces the whole of life, but I have chosen to limit my book to relatively few aspects and, in Part 2 especially, to love between man and woman and love of the child. In this respect, my book is, of course, artificial, since human growth takes place in the whole of our lives — our interpersonal relationships, our student and professional life, our leisure activities, the social environment in which we live and so on.

But it would be foolish to try to cover the whole spectrum. So I decided to limit my description of the movement of the inner life, that of the heart, to the search of so many young people for their future home and to that of older people for the roots of their love, which may have become difficult.

Difficulties — yes, I know I have stressed these in my book. This is in reaction to the attitude of so many young people who are setting out on their life of love as though it were a pleasure trip. They see the life of love as very easy. You are mutually attracted to each other and you respond to this impelling need. You just let it happen!

And then I have met so many people who are very disappointed because they have idealised love without being fully conscious of its difficulties. They have come up against all kinds of obstacles and have been very hurt. 'It has not been what I thought it would be,' they have told me in deep despair.

3

So I have tried to show that love is a beautiful but difficult Adventure that takes place throughout the whole of our life and is only fully unfolded in our definite encounter with God-Love.

Loving is not simply letting yourself be carried along by a wonderful feeling. It is supported and often raised up by that feeling, but it is above all wanting with all of your strength and even at the cost of your own life to give happiness to others or to one other.

It may be possible to use fear to make people obey a law, but fear will never lead anyone to love. So I have to disappoint those — very few, I hope — who would have liked me to speak of sin and the flames of hell. If I have lit a flame at all, I hope it is the flame of love.

My own limitations

Putting the poetry back into love and helping others to sense the infinite depths of its mystery! That is an ambitious, even a very pretentious aim! I am well aware of the great gulf between my aim and my own limitations. To produce a really perfect book would take longer than my life, which is in any case so very active. It would also require a great poet and mystic — someone with a pure enough faith to be able to see, in the hearts of those who try to love, a sign made by the living God.

And I am neither a poet nor a mystic. Like you, I am just trying to love and do not always succeed. So please just take this book as an attempt. I was asked to write it. I followed my usual practice and had it checked while I was writing it to see whether my words were having the right effect.

I have to thank with all my heart all those who helped me so much during the writing of this book with their comments and encouragement. I think I would have given it up without their help. Many of them were young people.

Finally, I am sure you will not be held back by the imperfections of the text and will not skim through it and over its surface in a single evening like a popular novel. You will read it as I have tried to write it — as slowly as possible and in depth and meditatively, going beyond my clumsy words in your own search for love. Then you may like to use the index at the end to find individual meditations on particular aspects of love.

Loving is a great Adventure — the greatest in life. In it, God is waiting for us.   *Michel Quoist*

Part I
Living is Loving

Friend, sit down
and listen to my story

Listen with all your heart!
If your heart is not open
you will only hear the sound of words
but will not taste their flavour.

1

I was twenty years old — or twenty-four or twenty-five, what does it matter!

I wanted to live, but I did not know how to live or why I was living.

I was searching!

My search was very painful. I seemed to be walking through a desert full of mirages.

I was hungry!

My body was hungry. My living flesh was like a thousand gaping mouths, eager to swallow even the tiniest fragments of pleasure found on the way.

My spirit was hungry. I fed it with all the words I heard uttered, all the ideas I could find in books and images and pictures of every kind. My head was like a beehive, buzzing with activity but producing no honey.

Sometimes, in the darkness of my activity, I was aware of a light shining outside my buzzing head, my body and my soul, a long way ahead of me, somewhere at the end of this world and at the beginning of a new universe. But as soon as the light came to me, it was obscured by clouds.

All that was left to me was my dream and that led me on.

But dreaming is not really living and the storm soon broke. My dream was shattered and I was left naked on my bed with nothing to protect me. I was like a man burning with love, but without a woman to be the object of that love.

I was thirsty!

My heart was thirsty. Deep within me, in the mysterious depths of my being, far deeper than my flesh and blood, I was thirsty. Trembling and uneasy, I was aware of my infinite thirst and of infinity.

7

My thirst was like a fire burning in an unfathomable pit, consuming me and setting light to everything that lived.

I went on living, but the question remained: How can I go on if I do not know how to live or why I am living?

My life was like a great parcel passed from one person to another, too heavy to carry and without a label, an object used by clowns to make people laugh. No one, least of all I, knew what to do with it.

My parents told me that they had done their duty, that they had 'given' me life as it had been given to them. They were generous and their intentions were good. They gave me moral teaching and I still had their 'directions for use', but these were almost impossible to read now. And had they ever really taught me how to read?

According to their directions for use, I had to do certain things and not do other things. But why? When I questioned my parents, they just said: 'Because this is right and that is wrong.' But they did not tell me why this was right and that was wrong. They themselves just did not know. When I pressed them for an answer, they just said: 'Because that is how it is.'

I soon noticed that they themselves did not always do what they told me to do. Nor did other adults always follow their own directions for use! My school friends laughed at me. 'Those directions are out of date,' they said. 'We do not know any others and, even if we did, they would be useless,' they assured me. 'You should not ask such questions because there are no answers.'

They went on: 'Why not just live? You can do anything you like now. There is no "Do not walk on the grass". You can go anywhere and gather as many flowers as you like from the flower-beds. Do just what you want to do and you will be happy!'

So I did what I wanted to do.

I went through many parks and gardens. I walked over the lawns and gathered the flowers of pleasure. But I did not find happiness. I caught a fleeting glimpse of it once or twice and tasted it for a moment or two, but it was like a sweet melting on my palate and leaving me still hungry.

And what about you, my friends? Do you too still experience the agony of hunger and thirst in your hearts? Or have you already given way to resignation? Have you become like the prodigal son in the Gospel? Have you left your Father far behind and gone off to become poor in spite of your rich inheritance, living on food stolen from the pigs?

Or are you like the dutiful son who has never left his Father's house and has continued to enjoy his bread and wine? Even so, have you never experienced hunger and thirst?

We are so made that hunger and thirst are never satisfied. That is our greatness and also our agony. I am quite certain of this. As soon as we think we have satisfied them, they are reborn and live even more vigorously within us. They even go ahead of us, moving so fast that the chase, which we cannot give up, exhausts us. But we never catch up with them. We *are* insatiable hunger and unquenchable thirst. We die when our hunger and thirst die.

I was hungry.
I was thirsty.
But I did not know what food and what drink I needed.
Nothing is worse than being hungry and not knowing bread.
Nothing is worse than being thirsty and not knowing wine.
I wondered who would set me free from my torture.

A friend told me: 'You will not find your way if you continue to look inwards at yourself. Go outside yourself! If you stay in the harbour you will never know the infinity of the ocean!'

Another friend said: 'Read the "Book". That will show you the way. It contains God's words and they are there to guide you on your way.'

I opened the Bible sometimes and found it easy to respect the words in it, because they struck me as beautiful, but their mysterious content escaped me. They were like grains of wheat with such a thick husk that I could not reach the life-giving germ inside.

A third friend urged me to find someone who would explain the meaning of the words to me: 'Someone who has eaten the germ and lives from it may be able to tell about the life those words give in the language of today.'

9

Then he said: 'Go and see the Sage. Every one says that he speaks like the Book and that his words are like seeds in the hearts of those who hear them. In good soil they bear fruit a hundredfold.'

So I decided to see the Sage.

I will tell you about my search, my doubts and my difficulties. It is a search I have made only with my heart — not with the whole of my life.

I will also tell you what the Sage told me — his words.

2

The Sage lived in a tiny flat at the end of a dark corridor. No one knew who he was or where he came from. The mystery of his being was respected by those who came to see him, including myself.

I groped my way along the unlit corridor, thinking: We have to go through darkness before we reach the light.

I knocked on his door. It opened and I saw him indistinctly in the dim light coming from a tiny window.

He was very old. I had foolishly imagined him with long hair and a long white beard, but no, his appearance was at first sight quite ordinary. Even his face, which I could not see very clearly, seemed ordinary. In fact, I could only really see his eyes — or rather, the light of his eyes. But I had an immediate impression that that light came from elsewhere. Its origin was mysterious, but I knew it was sun and life. If I let it enter me, it would, I knew, illuminate my everyday journey through life.

Later, of course, I had doubts about this.

He greeted me as a friend and stood looking at me for a long time. It was as if the morning dew was penetrating into the parched soil of my heart. After a long silence, he said in a quiet voice: 'You are very lucky.'

'Why do you say that?'

'Because you are human and you can search. A rose is beautiful, but it spends its whole life as a rose without knowing why and for whom it is beautiful.'

'What value is the search if you do not find?' I asked at once.

'Everyone who searches faithfully will find, but sometimes we are blind and reject the light or deaf and refuse to hear the word.'

It was then that my longing was irresistibly expressed as a fervent plea: 'Help me to live! I am hungry and thirsty for life and I cannot find anything that will satisfy me.'

The Sage did not move. He remained silent for a long time. Silence filled the room. It seemed to me that he was in a sense mysteriously wedded to silence and later he told me this was true, saying that silence had given him all the children that he had failed to receive from noise. 'You will come to love silence,' he said, 'and it will give you children too.'

But I had not come to see him to learn about silence. My world was full of noise. I took words with me wherever I went. They were the furniture filling the lonely, empty room of my life. I wanted words from the Sage.

'I want to live!'

Very quietly and very slowly, he replied: *'It is a question not so much of living as of loving.'*

I was on the point of asking him why, but said nothing. I was afraid his reply would be the one I had heard so often in the past — a reply like the sound of a door being slammed in my face: 'Because that is how it is!'

But I was wrong. He answered my unspoken question.

'Listen, my boy. Your obsession with your hunger and thirst is leading you astray. You will never satisfy them. Even if you had access to all the food and drink in the world and consumed them every moment of the day, you would still experience hunger and thirst. They are not your real hunger and thirst. They conceal another hunger and another thirst and those hidden longings are more persistent and more demanding, because they are infinite.

'The deepest longing in the heart of every man and woman is not the longing to live, but the *longing to love and to be loved*. That is what we are all hungering and thirsting for.'

He paused for a while, reflecting and then added in a low voice, as though he were speaking to himself: 'That is not surprising. We are, after all, made by love and for love.'

'But life comes first,' I objected. 'No one can love if that person is not alive first.'

'No,' the Sage said. 'No one can live if not loved first. Life is a river, not the source! As for you:

12

You plunge into the river and the water flows around you,
                but you cannot seize hold of it.
The living water will not obey you — you try to grasp it,
                but it slips through your fingers.
You climb onto the bank, drawn by a wild flower with
                fire-coloured petals,
then return to the water, only to find that it has been
                flowing without you,
leaving you behind, holding a dead flower.
You are tired now and stay in the middle of the stream
       contemplating the mystery of the ever-moving water.
You watch it flowing, flowing — but you cannot penetrate
   its mystery, beccause you do not know its origin and its
                destiny,
the Source and the Ocean.

So much for life!' the Sage continued. 'It flows like a stream in us and in the whole of mankind, because it comes from its Source. And *that Source is Love.*

'If you really want to live, do not try to hold the river of life back. That is something you cannot do in any case! Let it flow past other banks and water other meadows, while you go back to the Source.

If you try to save your life and to lock it up in your heart
             for your own enjoyment, you will lose it.
But, if you decide to lose your life in your search for the
             Source, you will find it.'

What the Sage had said had fascinated but disturbed me. My instinctive reaction was to argue.

'Lose my life! But I want to live, not to die!'

'I was not speaking of death. I was speaking of life.'

His last words, before I left without knowing whether I could come to see him again, were: 'One day you will know that *dying is not ceasing to live, but ceasing to love.*'

3

I had come home from work and was lying on my bed, as I so often did, like a ship with a leaky hull left in the harbour waiting to be repaired. I too felt in need of repair.

Almost a month had gone by since my visit to the Sage. I was attracted to him and curious, but also afraid to go again. I could not decide whether to revisit him and I was looking for excuses whether or not to go. Intellectually, I could not accept what he had said. Had he really answered my questions? In my heart, I was deeply uneasy and even fearful. I sensed danger and wanted to run away. I knew that what my heart was whispering was: The Sage's words are words of truth.

It is not difficult to muffle the whispering of one's heart! Noise is a powerful ally. I filled my room with the sound of music, turning up the volume until the memory of those words was overcome.

But I was still uneasy. I sensed the approach of the storm that I knew and feared so much.

When it broke it was the most violent I had ever known.

It came down on me like a tornado. I had tried in the past to build up some structures consisting of clear ideas and good intentions, I thought, on my little island, but they were torn down in a flash. Nothing within me remained standing. Everything was in ruins.

My heart seemed to be beating in a terrible emptiness and only just beating because it was mortally wounded by a deep feeling of absence. But a lack of what? Of whom?

I wondered in my tortured state whether I was abnormal, even mad. But is it madness to search for life? Is it madness to try to find the origin and destiny of life? Then I asked myself a question that I had never asked before: Is it madness to look for the value of life? Then, unable to prevent the tears coming into my eyes, I thought: If a thing is of no value, it is thrown away.

By now I was crying. For how long I do not know.

Why is it that so many men are ashamed to cry? I only know that I have seldom cried, but that every time that I have shed tears I have felt refreshed and that flowers whose presence within me I had not suspected have opened up.

The storm had passed and gradually calm returned and with it the gentle whisper of the Sage's words. I knew now with certainty that it was his words that had been troubling me so much that I had felt compelled to fight against them.

And I also knew I would go on fighting against them! I would not give up my life for a mirage!

I wanted to live and I would go on searching for life. I would pursue it, whatever the cost, find it and grip it in my fists. I would squeeze it with all my strength like a fruit to obtain its juice. I would make it yield up its happiness to me! Even if I harmed myself in the process.

I got up from my bed and went to the window. I opened it to call to the wind to come to me.

But that was my great mistake!

Through the open window came the sound of a song. An old love song. Sentimental, of course! But it was about love. Like all songs, like all films and all novels. They all speak of love. Like all people! And that song that spoke of love penetrated to my heart.

Looking out, I saw the people in the street. They were going back to their homes — to their love. Just as their love had made them leave their homes this morning to earn money or to buy food.

But some of those people were not going home to their love. They were going out, weary and disappointed because their love was dying or dead, hoping to find or even buy another.

Later that evening, young people would also be passing my window on their way home after having flirted with love in the belief that they were mastering it. Then the curtains would be drawn along the street and in each house or apart-

15

ment people would be trying to take hold of and eat a few morsels of love.

Parents and children, husbands and wives, married couples and single people, young and old, they would all in their different ways be looking for a few fragments of love. In their gestures, their words and their silences, their laughter and their tears, their dreams, their prayers and their blasphemy and in their warm embraces and their violence to each other. Trying to express a love that gives life. A love without which, I was beginning to know, we die of hunger.

But it was still light enough to see the people in the street.

A child was about to run across without looking and his mother threw herself forward to pull him back from the traffic.

I heard her say, so I thought: 'I would give my life for you,' but the words were in my heart.

A young man and woman were kissing tenderly and smiling and talking to each other.

I heard them say, so I thought: 'I would give my life for you,' but the words were in my heart.

A man was reading the headline in his newspaper: 'Another hunger striker dead'.

I heard him say, so I thought: 'I would give my life for justice and peace,' but the words were in my heart.

Then there was silence, a great deep silence, and through it, after a long time, I heard a voice. It was the Sage's voice.

He said: *'Love is more precious than life.'*

Had I been won over? Not yet, I think. But I went to bed at peace with myself and strangely-happy.

I was soon asleep and dreaming that I was knocking on the door of the Sage's flat.

4

I was not dreaming this time when I knocked on the Sage's door. I had hesitated for several days, partly because I felt that going to see him again was giving way to someone or something stronger than myself and I just do not like losing!

But an even more important reason for not going was that I was afraid — of being drawn into an unknown experience that I did not want and being taken along strange new ways. I felt very uneasy and wondered what the Sage would say to me after such a long absence.

All that he said was: 'Sit down, my son. You must be tired.'

'Why do you think I am tired?'

'Because fighting against oneself is very tiring. Many people use up such a lot of their strength and waste such a lot of time doing that. They continue the inner struggle for years, wearing themselves out, tearing themselves apart, leaving shreds of their lives on the way. And in the meantime their happiness takes flight.

'Others — and their case is much more serious — try to seek flight from the struggle that is taking place inside them. They look for distractions and are sometimes so successful that they cease to hear the noise of their struggle. At least during the daytime! But you cannot find activities to distract you during the night and so you suffer even more terribly then — and in silence.

'But you can be sure of this. Taking on the struggle — and admitting defeat — is not weakness, but strength.'

The Sage looked at me for a long time. I found it difficult to meet his eyes. I knew he could see into my heart, but I was proud and thought: If he is to understand me, I want it to be from what I tell him about myself. So I decided to speak openly to him.

I told him about the 'storms' in my life — those storms that brewed for so long within me without breaking, as on a summer evening when the air is stifling and heavy, and then tore me apart with their steel blades of fire.

I talked for what seemed hours. More than I had ever talked in the past. He listened to me, without moving, recollected and quite silent. It was above all his silence that set my captive words free.

But much of what I wanted to say about myself was too deeply buried within me and I fell silent, unable to raise the stone over the tomb of my heart.

He remained where he was, still listening. He seemed to listen even more attentively to my silence than to my words, but I knew he wanted me to go on talking. When he saw the first sign of new words on my lips, his eyes met mine and at once a bridge was built between us.

While I was speaking, I found myself thinking: Why are there so few people who can listen as this man does? So many words, perhaps of great importance, rot away in the tombs of our hearts — words and cries which might have aroused an echo in the hearts of others who were hungry and thirsty.

People die without ever having truly expressed themselves. That thought came to me with great force now, because it reflected my own experience. How many times in the past I had wanted to talk, but had remained silent! In reply to the sincere question: 'What are you thinking?' I had so often said: 'Nothing,' believing, often wrongly, that the questioner was trying to make me speak and betray myself.

Sometimes I had yielded, of course, but the words that had been pulled out of me were plants with strong, deep roots and had grown again just as vigorously and filled my heart again with their foliage and fruit, making it impossible for me to breathe and to see clearly.

But with the Sage it was different. I knew in my heart I could tell him everything with complete safety. I found myself smiling.

'Why are you smiling?' he asked at once.

'Because I am setting myself free,' I replied.

18

'You have just discovered a very deep truth, my son,' he said. 'Many people just do not know themselves because they proudly believe they can give birth to themselves. The fact is that none of us can reveal ourselves to ourselves unless we first reveal ourselves to another who listens to us with love.

'But it is getting late. Come back tomorrow and it will be my turn to speak to you.'

5

This time, the Sage spoke. I listened. Now that I was free of my own words, I had more room in my heart for his.

'You are beginning to understand,' he said, 'that love comes first in man's heart and man can give up his life so that love will live. As long as you remained imprisoned within yourself, you experienced those storms that you described to me. You were not able to speak without someone to listen and you have been cut off from love.

'The other evening, when the storm broke within you and you suffered so much, if a true friend had come and smiled and said: "I need you — for myself and for others," the storm clouds would have disappeared and you would have seen the sky again. But no such friend came.

'The loneliness of people closed in on themselves — what a terrible illness it is! It is a cancer attacking the heart and spreading over the whole of our being.

'In our society individuals have enclosed each other in a
          great city where they live together like bees in a hive.
They are confined within their little boxes close to the
          ground or reaching up to the sky in high-rise flats.
Imprisoned, they suffer and are lonely, brushing against
          each other only in the streets of the city.

Families are soon broken up, no longer alive and life-giving.
Their limbs, torn off, have made wounds that will not and
          can't stop bleeding.
Men and women who think they are so united to each
          other that they are one flesh
are only two sad separate and lonely beings lying side by
          side in the same bed.

20

So many countless travellers on the high seas are unable to
find a port of call
where they can share out with each other the gold that
they have taken from the coffers of their hearts.
They are simply adrift, driven by the winds, and all they
can do is to send out signals of distress —
signals that are just not seen or else are ignored by others
who say, but not, of course, aloud:
"I cannot go out. It is too dangerous at sea. And it is too
cold outside and I love the warmth."

People who claim to have been set free from all the old
taboos hope to be able to communicate with others,
but only come in fleeting contact with other bodies,
never reaching other hearts.
Some are silent, others speak, throwing words in each
other's faces.
Some dream of close encounters with others, taking them
home to the warmth and intimacy of the heart,
but in reality they all stay in their own homes with their
own dreams.

And while all this is happening,
children cry in their search for someone they can call
"father",
sick people call out in their suffering and are not heard
and old people are unbearably lonely at the end of their
lives.
We pay to keep them and our consciences quiet, as though
we did not know that nothing is so healing as a kiss.

Isolated in one way or another from each other,
more and more of us are imprisoned in our terrible
loneliness,
in a world of crowds,
in a world of stretched out arms
in a world of splendid thoughts and fine feelings,
in a world campaigning for justice and peace,
in a world of science and technology.

**Although our world offers so much that is positive and good,
we will never escape from our prison of loneliness
if we do not know how to love, and are not loved.**

'Well, my son', the Sage concluded. 'Now you are beginning to understand, why not make the effort to love? You will save your brothers and sisters and you will also save yourself.'

I did not reply. I was afraid·to say: 'Yes.'

Very gently he insisted: 'Make the effort!'

He went on: 'Open yourself to others! You cannot even hear them calling to you now, but so many people are only waiting for you to open yourself to them.

'Go out of yourself! You need others. You are very impoverished and the only way for you to become rich is to find a share in their lives; like that, you will make them rich, too.

'Make the effort,' he said again, 'and you will find that, as soon as you open the door of your heart to others, the sun will shine in. As long as you do not love, you will be in darkness, but, as soon as you love, you will be in the light.

'Yes. I will make the effort,' I said.

Quite spontaneously, like a parachutist jumping from an aircraft into space because the trainer is watching, I promised the Sage, because he was looking steadfastly at me, to try to love.

His reply was simply: 'Thank you — for yourself and for others.'

I did not understand what his 'thank you' meant.

6

Yes, I would and I did make the effort — several times.

It gave me a taste of happiness. That must have been the Sage's 'sun shining into my heart'. I felt less isolated and less troubled and for a little while, my heart was quite light.

But the Sage had spoken about love and what did I know about it? What he had said described something that was still a long way from my experience!

One day, soon after my visit to the Sage, two things happened that seemed to be related to what he had described.

At work, I was given a paper containing details of a union meeting. I usually glanced at those papers and then forgot the meeting, glad that I was not free to attend that evening. But this time, without knowing precisely why, I went.

An appeal was made to take part in action supporting a group of workers and I volunteered. Later, I was asked to help again. This time I did not agree so quickly. Where would it lead me? To what unknown country? And what benefit would I derive from it? Would my thinking of others make anyone think of me?

But I forced myself to say yes this second time and take part in the union action. But was forcing oneself to love really loving? I knew I would not do it again.

The other event concerned one friend. He needed to talk about himself and his problems and, although I wanted to talk about myself, I remembered what the Sage had said and listened to him.

My friend was obviously very happy and told me before he went home that he had spoken to me about worries that he had never before confided in anyone.

But a little later, he came to me again with his problems

23

and I reacted as I had reacted to the second appeal to help my union colleagues.

It was not difficult to find excuses for myself, but I still felt uneasy and troubled. I felt that I had been defeated. The Sage had deceived me, led me on against my will by his strange power over me.

That power was just in his eyes. He had just looked steadily at me while saying very ordinary things and his look had given me a sense of peace and had at the same time invited me to go out of myself. His eyes had seemed to speak of love and, while leaving me quite free, had nonetheless exerted an irresistible pressure on me to respond to their appeal.

But it was not long before the clouds began to pile up on my too low horizon and obscure the sun that I so much wanted to shine into my life and into my heart.

I had fleetingly experienced the light that the Sage had spoken about, but that brief glimpse was enough to make the darkness even deeper when it returned.

I was uneasy and profoundly disappointed. I felt resentment against the Sage and vowed to tell him about my feelings.

7

On my way to the Sage, I had thought of many fine things to say in praise of myself, but when he opened the door, the only words that came to my lips were: 'It is hard to love.'

His reply was simple and direct: 'Much harder than you think.'

I found myself making excuses: 'But I really have tried!'

He looked at me with that steady, penetrating gaze and I knew that he understood me better than I understood myself. There was no trace of sarcasm in his voice.

'Did you make those efforts to please me? Like a little child trying to please his mother? When we are grown up, we have to make efforts for ourselves. We have to be responsible for our own lives.'

'But I did not ask to be born. I did not give life to myself.'

'Of course not,' the Sage replied at once, 'None of us gives life to himself. We all receive life as a gift. And living is first of all accepting the gift of one's life.'

After a pause, he went on:

'How many people fail to live fully human lives because they have never learned to say 'yes' to their own life. Accepting your own life also means gathering its fruits and making them grow. A tree is not responsible for its fruits, but we human beings are. If we reject that responsibility, we are not fully human.'

I had a sudden insight.

'Is that why you said, when I decided to make the effort to love, "Thank you — for yourself"?'

Yes,' he replied simply.

'But you also said, "and for others". Why?'

When he replied, he spoke for some time.

'Because others are hungry and thirsty and you owe them the fruits of your life. If you just gather their fruits without offering them any of your own, you are behaving like a para-

25

site. Millions of human beings — women, men and children who are, with us, members of the one body — suffer terribly because so many feed on the lives of others but do not feed them with their own lives.

'I have read hundreds of books — of psychology, sociology, economics and political science — in an attempt to set my troubled mind at rest. But I eventually came to the conclusion that the one essential book that was missing from my library was the book of life.

'It was only when I began to look around me at life that I came to a deeper understanding of reality. Ideas without life, I realised, are no more than bones without flesh.

'I learned that it is possible to speak about very serious problems in very simple words. Too simple, I imagine, for many well educated people, but words that are illuminating for those who hear or read them with the ears and eyes of their heart.'

What the Sage had just said made me very happy, because this was the first time that he had spoken a little about himself. His words had also in a different way been illuminating for me.

He had also made me aware for the first time of the books covering the walls of his room. He was obviously a scholar, but he did not speak like one. And I was also aware that he too had searched, in his own way, and that it had been a very long and probably painful search. This gave me strength and encouragement.'

'You see,' he said, suddenly interrupting my reflection, 'I know a great deal now not just with my intellect, but also with my heart and the whole of my life.'

And he told me then of some of what he knew.

'If millions of men and women die of hunger while others
                    are dying because they eat too much,
it is because we have not yet learned to share our wheat
                    and our bread with each other.

If countless young people break out in violence and try to
                    take by force the things they are deprived of,
it is because their birth was a mistake, the result of a
                                        physical embrace
or of a desire to have a child after satisfying the desire for
                    furniture, a car and a pet dog.

If this earth is for a few people property and profit, and for
    so many no more than a place of exploitation or hardship,
it is because some have forgotten that it is for everybody,
                    not just the strongest or the richest.

If millions of people live without being able to take part in
    freedom and responsibility in building up the world,
It is because some think they were born to be masters in
        need of slaves to keep them in a position of power.

If the world is full of prisoners, many of them crying out
                        under torture,
it is because men who want to suppress critical thinking
believe they can do so by inflicting physical pain and death.

But I also know that there are men and women everywhere
                who have overcome their fear
and I admire them for risking being hurt in the great
                    struggle for justice and peace.

Yet you can throw your body into the struggle and can
                    even let your blood flow,
but that struggle will be in vain and there will be no
                    victory if the heart is not in it.'

The Sage paused, but I said nothing, sensing that he had
not quite finished.
    'Yes, I know all this and so do you, although you may not
want to admit it yet.
    'Learn how to look and listen. Look at human beings and
their suffering, the blood that they shed on the long way of
the cross of history. Listen to that great cry that rises from
the earth — "I am thirsty!"'
    Then he said something that I knew but above all did not
want to know:
    We are all of us responsible for suffering humanity.

27

8

Yes, I knew! I had, after all, looked and listened.

How is it possible to avoid looking and listening when you are assaulted every day by pictures and words reminding you of your suffering and oppressed fellow-men and women?

But I could not accept that I was responsible for that suffering. It was surely not my fault that I had a home and regular meals, that I was not illiterate and that I was fully employed. But, although I told myself resolutely that I was not responsible for it, I still felt the world's suffering as a sharp reproach.

Yes, I had looked and listened, but I did not want to look and listen any more. I could not bear what I saw and heard.

So I closed and locked the doors of my heart.

But how foolish it was to think I could shut that suffering out! I began to recognise the presence deep within me of a charge of dynamite that was only waiting to be detonated. And one day the pictures and words were so dramatic and painful that the explosion occurred in my heart and mind. My feelings and thoughts were broken into fragments and thrown into total disorder.

When I calmed down and began to gather up the pieces I knew all that suffering was not only atrocious, but also unjust.

At once I looked for something or someone to blame — society, governments, religion, God, teachers, the media, the capitalist economy, the uneducated masses who do nothing and can do nothing constructive . . .

I was in a state of revolt. I had picked up the pieces, but I had not really put them together again. The more I rebelled, the more proud I was of myself. I was not closed any more! I was no longer insensitive to the suffering of others!

My solutions to the problems of world poverty and oppression were radical. We all had to give much more to various kinds of aid! The political and economic structures had to be changed! We had to urge our government to act!

I began to talk vehemently and boldly about my solutions to my friends and colleagues, to everyone I met. I spoke with supreme confidence, reducing my listeners to silence and thinking that they admired me for my noble feelings and my eloquence.

My ideas and my words were good. My dreams were even better! Sometimes I saw myself leading a victorious crusade against poverty and oppression in the Third World and at others I dreamed that I was tenderly caring for a starving or sick child.

At night, I fell asleep very quickly after such thoughts, because I had put my conscience to sleep.

But it did not stay asleep for long.

Very soon it began to trouble me and it was not long before I was in turmoil again. Occasionally, at times of great silence, I became aware of its voice murmuring deep within me. That was above all why I hated and feared silence! At those times, I heard again and again the quiet words: 'What are *you* doing?'

At once, without a moment's reflection, I replied: 'What *can I* do about it? The world is so vast and its rulers are so powerful. And I am so insignificant! I would do something, but what use would it be if others do nothing?'

I replied quickly and loudly because I did not want to hear that dangerous inner voice.

I said: 'I would do something, but . . .' but in fact I did *nothing*.

The Sage had spoken to me about himself and myself and I had listened to him despite myself. I wanted to — had to — see him again. I had questions to ask him. But once again I hestitated to go. I was, I think, more afraid of his eyes than of his words.

I had a brilliant idea! I would write to him.

I did not post the letter. I do not know why, but, although it was very late when I finished it, I walked to his flat and slipped it in his letter box, leaving as quickly and as quietly as I could.

I was afraid that he might open his door.

29

9

The Sage's letter arrived the next day.

He must have written and posted it the same night he received mine.

My first feeling was one of pride — that he should have written to me so quickly. He thought highly of me! He liked me! Perhaps it was even that love of which he had spoken.

I felt warm and my heart glowed — but only for a little while. Very soon my euphoria was overshadowed by doubt. His love for me was because he had to love. Out of duty! He had to love because he required others to love.

Why, then, did I find myself trembling when I opened the envelope?

It was quite a short letter:

'If each note of music were to say: one note does not
make a symphony,
there would be no symphony.
If each word were to say: one word does not make a book,
there would be no book.
If each brick were to say: one brick does not make a wall,
there would be no house.
If each drop of water were to say: one drop does not make
an ocean,
there would be no ocean.
If each seed were to say: one grain does not make a field
of corn,
there would be no harvest.
If each one of us were to say: one act of love cannot save
mankind,
there would never be justice and peace on earth.

'In your letter you wrote: "What can I do? I am so insignificant."

'My reply is: *Love!* Not just in word or speech, *but in deed and truth*. Let it be real and active! Only love can overcome suffering. Even if you never see the fruits of the love that you give, it will act like a transfusion of new blood in the veins of humankind bleeding to death.

"But what use is it for me to do something, if others do nothing," you asked.

'My reply to that question is: They must love too!

'And you will say at once: They will try to avoid loving.

'In that case, you yourself must love all the more. Then those around you will love. They are like you — waiting for someone else to place the first stone. They will place their stone if you place yours and the house will be built. *The one who loves makes others love!*

> The symphony needs each note
> The book needs each word
> The house needs each brick
> The ocean needs each drop of water
> The harvest needs each grain of wheat
> The whole of humanity needs you
>   as and where you are
>   You are unique
> No one can take your place.

'Begin now! Why are you waiting?'

10

I read and reread my friend's letter.

He was right, of course, in what he had said. I had to begin now. Play a part, however insignificant that part might be, in building up the world and in helping to save my fellows. Why was I still weighed down by doubts and hesitating?

The fact was, I still could not accept myself as a single drop of water in the ocean, a single grain of wheat in the harvest. I wanted to be more than that and do more. But in the meanwhile, I continued to do nothing.

And meanwhile too, time was passing and I would never be able to make up for it. I had made use of all that past time for my own profit. I had not used it in the service of others.

I had tried to be blind to the pictures of human suffering I had seen, and deaf to the cries of men and women in pain. But that had proved impossible. The pictures and the cries had entered my heart and would not go away.

But even now I still looked for an excuse. Instead of asking: What *can I* do? I changed the emphasis and asked myself: *What* can I do? If someone were to come to me, I thought, with a concrete suggestion for action, however insignificant, I would carry it out.

Once again I went to see the Sage.

There was no sign of condemnation or even unfavourable judgment in his eyes. On the contrary, he was so kind and inviting that I felt immediately at my ease.

He waited for me to speak first.

I did not want to begin because I was still looking for the right words to open the conversation and set the tone. But when I at last commenced to speak in what had by now, I felt, become an oppressive silence, my words seemed shy, awkward and commonplace. I was ashamed of myself and wanted desperately to withdraw them.

'Thank you for your letter . . .' I murmured.

'I would have preferred to hear you and speak to you,' he replied very gently.

Once again I began looking for an excuse. I could hardly tell him I was still afraid of him — and above all of his eyes and the light they made shine in me, of his calm gaze that made me penetrate the mist that kept me a prisoner in my self-satisfaction.

'I did not want to disturb you . . . You are so busy.'

He smiled and I knew that he did not really believe my reason for not coming. But he spoke as though he had believed it.

'You never disturb me. The time I give to you is time *for you* — a little bit of my life given to you.'

He was very disarming! I decided to ask him the questions that had been on my mind.

'How am I to know who I should become? Who I should be?'

'By growing,' he said at once.

'Think of a tree growing,' he went on. 'Imagine that it is like a human being and conscious of itself. It would only discover very gradually what it was becoming or should become — a plane-tree, an oak or a poplar. If it was a plane-tree and wanted to be an oak or if it was an oak-tree and wanted to be a poplar, it would never succeed and would only be unhappy.

You must become and *be yourself*. You can let others make you richer, but you should never copy them. Others have need of you — of the you yourself that you must be. Never act the part of your life. You may succeed brilliantly in the role that you are playing, but others do not need that — they need your life.'

'How am I to know what I should do?' I asked him.

'By growing

as and where you are
at the time when you are there
with the people around you.'

He paused for a moment, then went on, as he had often
done before, in a kind of poetic meditation spoken aloud.

'By growing like a tree,' he began and continued, as if he
were addressing the tree of his thoughts:

'Tree — heavy, firm and beautiful!
Send your roots down into the earth,
    because, without them and the earth,
    you cannot live.
Send your branch-roots up into the sky,
    because, without them and the sky,
    you cannot survive.
        Let your earth-roots
        and your sky-roots
        eat and drink
        humus and water,
        air and sun.

Tree, my friend, grow for yourself,
    grow for me,
    grow for all men!
We need you
    so that we can breathe
    and keep warm,
    build our homes
    and furnish them,
    so that we can sleep
    and love each other,
    live and die.

Tree, you are not alone!
    You stand with countless others
    in the depths of the forest.
You stand with your sisters,
    listening to the sounds of the city,
    the laughter and tears of men and women.
Your branches are stretched wide
    like arms to welcome those
    who come to you for shelter.

They make you fertile
and you give them life.

But, tree, be yourself!
　Do not receive the predators
　who come to exploit you
　for their profit or pleasure.
If your heart is fashioned
　into the roof of a home,
do not let it be burnt
　so that men may keep warm.
If children play
　in the shade of your branches,
do not let yourself become
　a student's desk
　or an old person's chair.
If one day you have to become
　an altar for a priest,
do not be a table for a family
　or a bed for lovers.

Tree, my sister!
　send your roots down into the earth
　and your branch-roots up into the sky.

'Be the tree you should be!
　But also be a tree for others!'
'My friend,' I said, when he had finished speaking, 'Much of what you said I did not understand. I would like you to explain it.'
'I am not going to give you an explanation,' he said, smiling. 'Live and grow. Ask your heart! Your heart will tell you what it means.'
Then, very quietly and looking down, as though he was speaking to himself, he added: 'I may have sown too much seed. If you sow too much, the seed will not grow.'
He looked at me again and said:
'I would like you to come back. We have so many words to sow in the ground that we really ought to make very many drills. You must prepare the soil. No seed will grow if the ground is not prepared.'

I stood up and went to the door, but he called me back.
'Remember:
Send your roots down into the earth
and your branch-roots up into the sky!'
He fell silent for a moment, then added in a low voice:
'But do you know your sky — your heaven?'

He closed the door behind me.
I was alone with his last question.

11

Very gradually what the Sage had been saying was becoming meaningful for me. His words were beginning to grow in my heart like seeds in the earth. Their growth was so slow that I was hardly aware of it, but I knew that their fruit was making me live.

I knew too that I was happy to be alive. That was something that I had not experienced for a long time! At the same time, I had a deeper and more true insight into the nature of my long and dreary reflections and my demented dreams. They were, I now saw, entirely negative. They had only consumed my strength and had given me nothing. They had deprived me of all knowledge of who I was and of all sense of direction in my life. They seemed to want to keep me in a vague but sombre state of unreality.

I was now above all conscious of the need to live. And if I wanted to live, I had to set myself free and rediscover the earth to which I belonged and my own roots in it.

I was determined to discover that earth and those roots. How foolish I had been ever to think I could ignore or reject that earth and those roots! To imagine that I could live at all without them!

I was an oak-tree, not a plane-tree or a poplar and I would be an oak. I was 'where I was' and I would grow where I was and bear fruit there, in that place, at that time and with those people around me.

My place was that part of the earth where I was now. That was my earth, where I had my roots, the reality of my life — my family, the people I met at work, in my neighbourhood and in my leisure activities, the people who surrounded me, the people I liked and those I did not like.

My time was the time at which I was living, the time that

included all the major and minor events that occurred in and around my life, that touched me directly or indirectly and appealed to me.

My mind was made up. I was and would continue to be 'where I was'. But a moment's reflection showed me that it was very difficult to be with my roots down into the earth and my branch-roots up into the sky.

In the sky?

The Sage had asked me if I knew my sky — my heaven.

What was my sky — my heaven, then?

I would find it — as he had said — by growing.

He had also said, quite truthfully, that I was not alone, but was with 'countless others', like a tree in the forest.

Up till now, I had known this, of course, but only with my mind. I had not known it with my eyes, my ears and my hands. If you only look at yourself, you cannot see others and, if you only listen to yourself, you cannot hear others.

Now, however, I was beginning to encounter those others and to come into contact with their lives.

And, as I came closer to them, I became more and more conscious of the appeals they were making. How long it had taken me to understand that such appeals were constantly being made all around me and very close to me and that my task should always have been to respond to them. It was only now that I was becoming aware how necessary — and how difficult — that response was. And often how ineffectual!

But I had resolved not to think any more about the enormous size of the field containing the crop to be harvested and not to forget that I was holding a single but unique and important seed to be sown. I had decided I would no longer talk vehemently about building a new world, but simply place my one valuable brick in position on the wall.

I would put what the Sage had taught me into practice.

I tried first of all to go out of myself and towards the others. But I discovered soon enough that the change that I wanted to bring about in my life did not move at the same pace as my understanding of myself and of the realities of my existence. The gulf between understanding and action could be either discouraging or challenging!

I chose to accept it as a challenge. I would fight!

I also decided not to look elsewhere for some other

battleground. Faithful to my rediscovery of the reality of my life, I would fight here — in the place where I was. That was clear evidence, surely, that I had changed radically already! I no longer did nothing in passive resignation because I was not the head of a great enterprise. I was, on the contrary, ready to do the smallest thing as a humble but unique member of the work force.

I knew exactly what I had to do today and I was quite sure that, if I did it faithfully, I would discover — by growing — what I would have to do tomorrow.

At the same time, I also decided to wait for a week or two before going to see the Sage again. I wanted to have my soil prepared first.

12

Some light, I realised, had entered my life, but there were great areas within me that were still dark. In my heart especially, I still feared the light and knew there was a danger that I would once again lose myself in the shadows, which I feared equally.

But there was some light now in my life and it drove me irresistibly on my way. I was glad to continue in that light along the path that I had begun to follow, despite the fear that haunted me — the fear perhaps that I would not be able to stop and turn back.

Some of the things that the Sage had said fascinated me, because I sensed that they hid some essential truth as a tree hides its sap — that life-giving force that is only revealed when the tree is hurt and the sap weeps out of the broken branch.

Above all I was fascinated by what he had said about love as the reason for our being. It was, I thought, the life-giving sap flowing deep within us. What the Sage had said during our first encounter, when he had spoken about the river of life, came back to me now: 'We are made by love and for love.'

But I was still a long way from sharing that conviction with him!

Had I been 'made by love'?

My mother had explained the 'mysteries of life' to me very clearly when I was quite young. She had taken to heart the ideas that were current at the time and had done it in such a natural way that I was not even aware of the mysterious nature of those mysteries.

Later, however, when I was adolescent, I learned that my

parents could have had a child without wanting one. They could have made a mistake. A child might have been the result of a moment of weakness or forgetfulness. That thought, I remember, was obsessive at the time and it tormented me: Had I been an unwanted child?

Then, later still, I learned something even more horrifying, so it seemed to me even at that age: we had acquired the 'right' to destroy the life that we did not want. It was possible for men and women to have only the children they wanted. They could erase their mistakes.

I had the impression that my father regarded that as a great victory. My mother expressed no opinion. I wondered fearfully, hesitating to ask myself the question and certainly not daring to answer it: if they had had that 'right' then, when I was expected, and it had cost them nothing, would I be here now?

How little adults know of what goes on in the heads and hearts of young people!

Now I was still confronted with the same question — are we made by love? — but I no longer applied it simply to myself. I was conscious of its much greater dimensions.

How was it possible to believe that the millions of children in the underdeveloped countries had been 'made by love' — those children who were condemned to die long before they became adults? Surely that was a kind of monstrous destruction of unwanted life — a collective abortion that should be publicly denounced.

And 'made for love' — how could I believe that people were made for love when so many of them spent their lives living for themselves while exploiting and destroying each other?

No, the Sage was wrong. I could not believe in the truth of his 'made by love and for love'.

And yet he was so obviously convinced of that truth. For him, love was essential to humankind.

Yes, I was beginning to understand that it could be the essential Energy deep within me that enabled me to continue on my way, living and struggling, the mysterious breath that made it possible for us to sacrifice our lives if the need arose. It was perhaps that mysterious hunger and

41

thirst that I was experiencing so painfully — that longing that was no sooner satisfied than it made itself felt again even more powerfully.

I had to admit it — I understood nothing. Nothing at all!

I and my fellow-men were just actors playing parts in an absurd and comic tragedy of immense proportions. If we were made for love, we were still incapable of giving or receiving it. We were condemned to an eternal longing that would never be fulfilled.

How poor and wretched the human race was! The victim of a horrible farce. How long would its suffering last? It would last for ever unless some mad or very brave person put an end to it by an act of total destruction. And such an act was possible now. That was perhaps the only hope — the hope of death.

But love! A fine childhood dream for right-thinking children!

I told the Sage all this when I went to see him.

The storm was rising in me again, that old familiar experience, and I secretly hoped he would calm it as I was describing my thoughts and reactions. I was afraid that my ship was too fragile to sail through the ferocity of the storm that was breaking and would return to the port from which it had set out so resolutely.

But he made no attempt to calm my inner storm. On the contrary, he joined me on the open sea and was tossed with me by the waves.

As I was talking about love and telling him of my doubts and my fears that made me rebel against it, he interrupted me quite brusquely. His face, usually so pale, became quite flushed. His eyes lit up with a fire that I had never seen before. When he spoke, his voice was quite loud and sharp. He is angry, I thought.

'You are right, my son. Too few people believe in love these days and for too many it is something to laugh and sneer at. The world has more to fear from those people than from terrorists, who are after all motivated, however strangely, by love. Those who have no faith in love and mock it are more dangerous.

'What is left of love in our world today?' he asked.

'In the past there were the cruel and destructive theories of
                                          the philosophers,
    penetrating into our minds and gradually killing even
                              our most firmly held convictions,
    but Love, however scarred, remained in our hearts.

There was poverty in the world, illiteracy, hunger and suf-
                                                          fering,
    but Love remained in our arms, a weapon to be used
    for life.

There was injustice and grotesque inequality, Freedom
                                    could barely survive,
    but Love remained, hidden deep in the hearts of
                                              prisoners
    and beyond the reach of the oppressors.

There was armed struggle and war, injury and death,
    but Love remained, in blood and tears, but still
                                            surviving.

There was madness and dangerous folly in the world,
    but Love remained —
    a mysterious and pure breath
    exchanged between lips touched by each other,
    and nests of entwined bodies
    wove nests of children.

But now the very heart of Love has been violated.

    Love is free love, which men and women make
    with their bodies, not with their hearts.
    Love is taught like physical education or a sport.
    Love is watched on the intimacy of the small screen
        between the advertisements for pet food and light
                                          entertainment.
    Love is also displayed on the wide cinema screen,
        a public spectacle of physical excitement and emotion.
    Love is in porn shops, on cassettes and in pictures,
        magazines, inflatable dolls and sex symbols
        for those whose home fires have gone out

and who seek a warmth they will never find
in the red light district.
Love is on sale in the streets
and is on the menu everywhere —
if you have no more money, you will get no more love.
Love is disfigured, distorted and sold for cash.
Love has been made into a thing
and bits of it are used
and then thrown into the dirt of the gutter.

Love remained . . .
but now all that remains of that love are dying embers,
while men and women are dying of cold
their lips trembling,
their eyes burning feverishly,
clutching in their shaking fingers
pieces of the thing that is still called "love".

'How wretched we are,' the Sage concluded, 'not knowing that *in killing Love we are killing life itself.*'

He was looking down now and not at me. Luckily, I thought, because I could not have endured the light in his eyes. When he looked up, I was astonished at the speed with which he had recovered that calm that had become so familiar to me.

All that he said was: 'It is sad, very sad. But I am sure that *Love will be victorious.* I believe that with all my heart.'

I was once again in a state of total confusion. The rays of light that had so recently shone into my life were obscured by an impenetrable fog and, however much I wanted to believe in what the Sage had been telling me, I still felt deeply divided in my heart.

The only word that can describe Love, I concluded, is 'mystery'. The mystery of life is the mystery of Love. It was unthinkable that that mystery should not exist. And that mystery was known to the Sage. Why, then, did he not reveal it to me?

13

The mystery of Love — I decided to set off in search of it.

After all, I knew nothing about it, apart from the little I had learned from the Sage.

My understanding of love — not its mystery — could be summed up in a few words. Married couples sometimes dreamed of it, but were often cruelly disappointed. Fathers could be forceful in their love for their children, and mothers tender. Friendship — I had looked for that form of love, but had often been disappointed. Desire for a girl — I had experienced that and had looked at many girls, hoping they would return my smile. I had kissed them in reality or in dreams, gently or violently, and touched them lightly or tried to hold them in my arms.

But surely Love was more than this! Surely it went beyond the experience of married couples, parents, friends or girls. Beyond a moment of happiness or a fleeting physical excitement.

> Was it my port of call in the night,
>   my undiscovered island,
>   my hunger and thirst,
>   my quest, my struggle,
>   my suffering and my wounds,
>   my sorrow and remorse?
>
> Was it my desire and my torment,
>   coming from an unknown origin
>   and going to an unknown destiny?
>
> No, I knew nothing about the mystery of Love.

When I saw him, the Sage told me:

'The mystery of Love goes far beyond love.

Love is the flight of a bird in the infinite sky.
   But the flight of a bird is
      more than a little body circling in the air,
      more than its loving wings loved by the wind,
      more than inexpressible joy when the beating of
                          wings is no longer heard
      and more than a body at peace hovering in the light.

Love is the song of a violin singing the song of the world.
   But the song of the violin is
      more than the instrument and its bow lying unplayed,
      more than notes in evening dress dancing on the score
      and more than the musician's fingers moving on the
                          strings.

Love is light on our way.
   But the light that lightens this journey is
      more than a caress in the morning opening the eyes
                          of night,
      more than rays of heat from a fire, warming our
                          bodies
      and more than a thousand silk brushes touching our
                          cheeks with colour.

Love is a silver river flowing down to the sea.
   But the river cascading swiftly or hardly moving is
      more than its welcoming bed, that case full of jewels
      more than sparkling water, red in the light of the
                          setting sun,
      and more than the angler on its bank, hoping the bait
                          will tempt its fish.

Love is a ship, sailing on the open sea.
   But the sailing-ship's course is
      more than its prow parting the waves that yield or
                          resist,

more than its nails beating in the high wind or flutter-
ing in the gentle breeze
and more than the sailor's hands gripping the tiller to
control his headstrong lover.

The mystery of Love goes far beyond love.

*Love is an infinite breath that comes from elsewhere and
goes elsewhere.*

Love is the human spirit and knows the Breath —
it is human freedom turned towards Him.

Love is each one's consent to the inviting *Breath* —
it is each one's heart open to receive and give Him,
it is each one's body, recollected and available
so that He can dwell and remain in it
and go to others and to the other,
so that in the end
what was far off can be brought back,
what was separated may not be alone
and the one new life may come into being.'

'Oh my friend,' I said when he had come to the end of his
meditation, 'Tell me who that Breath is,

that Breath who is so mysterious and powerful
and for whom I have been waiting for so long,
and I will open my heart to Him
and give Him my body,
so that my joy may live
and my life may live!'

The Sage sat for some time in silence with his eyes closed
and in a state of deep recollection.

His silence did not make me feel uncomfortable. Quite the
reverse! I knew now that this was the dawn. The sun was
rising, but today it was taking longer than usual.

I looked at my friend and was astonished by his face, very
serious, but as expressive as ever, even though his eyes were
closed. He was quite motionless.

Then I saw that his lips had begun to move, almost imperceptibly. Was he speaking in a soft voice?

His features gradually relaxed. A slight quiver passed across his face. I was reminded of the breeze moving over a field of corn, but this went deeper, for his face seemed to change, becoming translucent, as though it was illuminated from within by a mysterious light.

After what seemed a very long time, he opened his eyes, looked very steadily at me and said:

'Pray, my son, Pray!'

He stood up and went with me to the door.

I left in silence, without even saying good-bye.

14

'Pray, my son. Pray!'

The Sage's parting words echoed in my mind. They did not surprise me, because I knew that the Sage must be a believer. He had never in fact spoken of God or his own faith, but the light that he had kindled in my heart and the strength that he had communicated to me could not have come simply from him alone.

Yes, I knew that he prayed, but did I also have to pray? Could I not penetrate to the depths of love without prayer?

Prayer and faith. Yes, I believed in God. Not just because my parents believed — my mother firmly and my father more vaguely. I believed because the alternative was absurd and meaningless. I just could not accept that I had come from nowhere and was going nowhere, that my life was the result of pure chance and that I was in the meantime hanging in a void.

And now the Sage's words about love had made my belief much less vague. I recalled my grandparents' very tender love for me and my love as a child for them. They were dead, but surely that reciprocal love could not be dead for ever!

I had often thought about these things very seriously, but always on my own. No one had ever accompanied me on my search. I had been an explorer, looking for the source of the river of life without companions, a guide, a compass or a map. But that was in the past. I had long ago given up the search in discouragement.

At least I believed that there was a Source. That was surely the important thing. Even if I knew nothing about that Source, I believed in it. Many people live like that. Their lives are not worse because they apparently never experience a longing to find the mysterious Source of life.

I tried to resign myself to passive, unquestioning acceptance, but from time to time I had heard what seemed to me to be a call to set off once again in search of my origin — my God. I had very often been conscious of this call when I was in a black and negative mood, weary with life because I did not know the reason for my existence, and then it had been irresistible.

But I also recognised that I had made some progress in my search. I was now looking not for something, but for *Someone*. I was like a child who did not know his father and who was driven by an overpowering urge to see his face.

What the Sage had said made me long with all my heart for that face to be the face of love, but that in itself created a difficulty, because that face was different from the face that I had given to the God of my own childhood. And I could not totally erase the memory of that face! That childhood god was still my God and I had to go on believing in him and living with him, even though I did not understand him or love him. I usually overcame this difficulty, not always successfully, by trying to forget both God and the search.

The God I believed in was omnipotent and absolute. He had power over life and death. He judged, condemned and rewarded. He gave and took away. He distributed good and evil in ways which defied understanding, but which were in my opinion certainly very unjust.

Above all, he let people suffer. He may even have made them suffer! Believers accepted suffering as 'God's will'. Belief did not mean that for me! So I concluded that, if I believed, it was not with the faith of a Christian.

But I tried to do what the Sage had suggested. I tried to pray. I tried to obtain favours from my omnipotent, absolute and — let me be honest — arbitrary and cruel God. I even believed once or twice that he heard my prayer. But for the most part, I encountered a terrible silence and was very discouraged.

But I had to admit that my contact with the Sage had resulted in a strange desire and an inexplicable *need* to pray. I was driven to look for God, but I did not want my God. So then I prayed:

50

'Because I believe you exist, my unknown God,
   make yourself known to me,
   silent God who troubles me.

I am praying to you today,
   but only because I need *Light* on my way
   and because I need *Love* —
   I need to be loved if I am to love.

My unknown God,
   I do not understand you,
   I feel resentment against you,
   I do not love you.
   But I want so much to love you!'

I was unaccountably afraid to address God in those simple
words. Perhaps I feared that it was blasphemous to do so.

The next time I visited my Friend I kept my eyes on his
face — that face that spoke to me even more clearly than his
words.

His happiness increased visibly as I told him about my
attempts to pray, and communicated itself to me.

'You have been praying very well, my son,' he said.

I was happy because he was happy. His happiness became
my happiness! It was like the coming of spring after a long
winter. But I still did not understand. What was happening in
me that was able to give me such happiness? I was still in
darkness.

The Sage divined my thoughts, as he divined everything
before I expressed it. When I had first known him, this had
irritated me, but now it pleased me. My friend welcomed
me and was glad just to have me with him. There was no need
for me even to speak.

'It is still night-time for you,' he told me, 'but it is Christmas
night. You should be glad, because the true God of heaven
and earth is being born today in your heart like a little child.

'He is coming to you and coming into you, because you
have said "*yes*" to him.

'Welcome him and love him.'

'I do not know him. How, then, shall I recognise him?' I
asked.

51

'Take off everything that covers your God, my son, for you cannot adore those clothes,' the Sage replied. 'Strip off his garment of absolute power and his judge's cloak. He has been in that disguise for so long that you cannot see him as he really is. It is legal minds that have dressed him up in those clothes, but you have added to their work with your wrong understanding, your imagination, your fears, your desires and your prejudices.

'Undress your god!' he went on, 'And, when you have taken off all the layers of worthless finery in which you have dressed the true God, you will see him with the eyes of your heart as he really is! *You will know that the true God has only one face — the naked face of Love. And that Love is Jesus Christ,*

> *naked* **in the manger**
> *naked* **on the cross.**'

The Sage fell silent and raised his head. He was looking straight ahead and I saw that his eyes were fixed on a beautifully carved crucifix on the wall in front of him. It was above all the face of this representation of the crucified Jesus that was so powerful — although dead, it seemed to be living beyond death.

So at last I had certain knowledge that it was in Jesus Christ that the Sage believed and that it was Jesus Christ whom he loved.

'Look,' he said after a long silence, looking not at me, but still at the face he loved.

'That is the true God who has gone ahead of us in Jesus Christ —

> **without human clothes,**
> **without human power,**
> **abandoned,**
> **despised,**
> **alone,**
> **naked,**

so that men and women may *believe that only Love can give life*, save it and make it flourish in eternal happiness.'

My friend ceased to speak. He lowered his head. Once again I was aware of his lips moving very slightly. I knew now that he was praying and I respected his prayer.

52

He continued to pray for a long time.

His silence did not embarrass me at all. On the contrary, it filled me almost to overflowing. I felt at peace, as if I were reposing inside the great silence. When it ceased, I came out of it, but was still deeply at peace.

The Sage broke his long silence with the words: '"Father, forgive them, for they know not what they do."

> 'They cannot recognise *Love*.
> They mock *Love*.
> The put *Love* to death
> yesterday, today and tomorrow
> in you and in your members.'

'"Father, forgive them, for they know not what they do." Forgive us

> and give us back *Love*.'

Once again he fell silent.

And once again he began to pray.

I lowered my head in order to look inwards and seek my inner life.

I think I prayed too because I heard myself saying in a whisper or maybe silently:

'Father, forgive me, for I did not know what I was doing.'

It was from that moment onwards that *I wanted to be forgiven.*

This time it was I who broke the silence.

'If it is really God you have been speaking about, I am ready to love him. How wonderful it would be if there were a God who is so near to us and who does not inspire fear.'

I was ready to love him, yes, but how could I really believe in a God who was so defenceless and poor and such a long way from the image I had of God, the God *in whom I believed but lacked the strength to love?*

'Go in search of other people, my son,' the Sage said.

'And continue to pray! For "no one can come to Jesus unless the Father draws him".'

53

15

He was drawing me — I was sure of that now. He had been
drawing me for a long time. Perhaps he had always been
drawing me.

He had been beckoning me. I knew now that he lay beyond
my hunger and thirst that could never be satisfied, beyond
my black moods and my negative periods, beyond my anger
and frustration caused by human suffering and man's injustice to man, and beyond my inarticulate longing for peace,
truth and love. Beyond all this, I was conscious of a sign
made by the living God, God who is Love, God-Love.

'No one can come to Jesus unless the Father draws him',
and he had been drawing me. But how could I ever encounter him? I was so firmly enclosed within myself! To meet
him, I had first to go out of myself.

I had tried to go out of myself, of course, but had
hesitated on the porch, afraid of the outside world.

The Sage had urged me: 'Go out in search of other people.'
He had pushed me out to follow my way of man. My way,
not the way of my ideas, dreams and fantasies! Nor the way
of my impressions, feelings and emotions! No, I had to
follow the way of my brothers and sisters, the people I would
meet every day in my daily life.

And everything that he had said pointed in the direction
of Love. I had to love my brothers and sisters, the people I
met on my way. In setting me on the way to my brothers
and sisters, he was setting me on the way to God.

'No one has ever seen God' — but he had taken on a *human
face* in Jesus. I did not fully understand this yet, but it was
gradually becoming clear to me that, since Jesus' coming
into the world, anyone 'who does not love his brother whom
he has seen cannot love God whom he has not seen'.

My search had been a long one, but it had been made spas-
modically and in darkness. I had followed the wrong path
and I had been looking for a wrong god! That at least was
clear to me now!

From now on, I had to look for God stripped of all the
useless finery covering him and seek him

naked in the manger
naked on the cross.

I knew now that I longed with all my heart to know and
love him.

I returned to the Sage and asked him to tell me more
about God.

'I will tell you more, my son, because you ask me to. But
first I must say this: We do not learn about God. He reveals
himself to us. I may be able to throw a little light on him
by what I say, but you will only encounter him and get to
know him *by living and loving.*'

'All the same, I would like you to tell me about your faith,'
I replied.

'The whole of my faith?

'If I told you about the whole of my faith now,' he said,
'you might understand with your intellect. But you are not
yet far enough along the way to be able to understand with
your heart.'

'I would still like you to tell me about your faith. I will
follow it at a distance with my heart.'

My friend smiled and said:

'**I believe that** *"God is Love".*
I believe that he is Family —
    Father, Son and Spirit,
    three Persons, so united by *Love*
    that they are only One.

I believe that God is infinite happiness
    because he is *infinite Love.*

I believe that his creation is the fruit of Love
    because Love wants to share its happiness.

I believe that, even before we exist,
    every person is loved
    personally and infinitely by God.
I believe that every person will always be loved by God,
    whatever he or she may say or do.
I believe that every person is conceived and made flesh by
                                      God
    and that the image of God in us may be disfigured,
    but can never be destroyed.
I believe that we are made by love and for love
    and that we are therefore free
    and invited to share in the infinite happiness of love.
I believe that God has given his creation to us,
    for us to work together
    to take possession of it and complete it
    and put it at the service of our fellow-men and women.
I believe that God has created us
    to be creative with him
    through the human family,
    which is the image of his Family,
    and to be free to make life come into being
    or to reject it.
I believe that 'God so loved the world that he gave his
                                  only Son',
    sending him 'into the world',
    so that infinite Love might, through Mary, take on
        a human face,
        a human body
        and a human heart
    in *Jesus of Nazareth*,
    who lived for thirty-three years
    in the centre of human history
    and covering the whole of history.
 I believe that Jesus,
    because he was man, was brother to each of us,
    and, because he is brother to each,
    is in solidarity with each one's sin,
    the sin of not loving.

I believe that Jesus,
   just as he endured his own suffering,
   endures the suffering of each one of us.

I believe that Jesus,
   in giving his life out of love for his brothers and sisters,
   has given back to every one of us
   and to the whole of mankind
   all the love that has been wasted by us
   and that, in restoring love,
   he has restored life to us.

I believe that Jesus
   has passed through death
   and lives among us
   and will be among us until the end of time,
   and that, through him and in him,
   we may live the life that has no end.

I believe that those who believe in and love Jesus
   together form one great people of God,
   the community of the Church.

I believe that this Church community,
   of which I am a member in Jesus
   with my brothers and sisters,
   is weak and sinful because of us
   and has not remained one because of us.

But I believe that it is still called
   to be one and holy
   and to be a sign of Love.

I believe that Jesus wanted people
   to be responsible for his Church
   and that, because they are human,
   they are weak and sinful
   and have made and are still making mistakes.

But I respect them and love them
   because Jesus wanted them, chose them and called them
   and because his Spirit has been with them
   throughout human history
   and is still with them.

I believe that the Spirit of Jesus, the *Holy Spirit*,
 is the *Breath of Love*,
 coming to meet every one of us —
 we are free to reject or accept him,
 to be open to him,
 to welcome him,
 to be pervaded by him
 and to be sent by him
 in search of others.

The Breath of Love unites us
 as individuals and as communities.
The Breath of Love unites man to the universe
 and builds up the Kingdom of God.

The Kingdom of God is a Kingdom of Love,
 rooted in our human history today
 so that it can spread tomorrow
 in the Love of the Trinity.

'And that is why, my son,' the Sage concluded, 'I believe
that, with Jesus Christ and in him,
 living is loving in the Breath of the Spirit.
 And I also believe that Love cannot die,
 because it comes from God
 and goes back to God.'

I had listened to him spellbound. What he had told me before his meditation was true, of course — I did not understand
because I was not yet far enough along the way. But I trusted.

I had a vision. In it, night was passing and dawn was breaking. I saw the sun rising slowly on the dark horizon and filling
the world, my world, with new light.

And I knew that he was my sun. He was 'the true light that
enlightens every man'.

He had risen in the darkness of my heart and in my heart I
had recognised him, even though I had not fully known him.

I was filled with great joy.

'My dear Friend,' I said, 'He is that mysterious Breath who
comes from elsewhere and goes elsewhere!'

'Yes, my son, that is who he is — the Holy Spirit, the Spirit of Love, God.'

'And is the Spirit of Love present when we love and are loved?'

'Yes, he is, just as the Sun is present in each one of its rays and the Source is present in each drop of water in the river.

'The rays of the Sun are not the Sun itself, nor is the river the Source. But there would be no rays of light and no river if there were no Sun and no Source, offering and giving themselves.

'*Love is greater than your heart and greater than your body. Love is the Breath of God* permeating our earth, entering the hearts and bodies of all people who love, just as he enters your heart and your body.

'God is love and all authentic love comes from God and goes back to God, passing on its journey through us, and we, because we are free, can reject that love or open ourselves to receive it and hand it on.'

'But,' I said, as a misgiving suddenly struck me, 'So many people do not know the God of Love. How is it possible for them to love?'

'The Sun's rays do not know the Sun and the river does not know its Source, but the world is full of light and the river is full of water flowing into the sea!

'So, my son, many people love their sisters and brothers without knowing they are filled with God's Love and without knowing the name or the face of the one they love when they are loving others.

'If they are faithful, they will know, perhaps much later, perhaps only when life breaks out beyond death — the life of the grain of wheat that has died because it has fallen into the earth. Then they will know and their eyes and ears will be opened and they will be told by Jesus: It was I.

'It was I — the one you fed when he was hungry
              longing for bread, dignity and friendship.

It was I — the stranger you welcomed,
              who did not belong to you, whom you loved.

It was I — the prisoner you set free,
        who had been kept in chains forged by human
                                                hands.

It was I — the one who was longing for you,
        the one you fed, welcomed, set free and loved
        when you gave yourself to others,
        though, not knowing me, you did not give
                                        yourself to me.

'And they will "inherit the Kingdom prepared from the foundation of the world", entering into the joy of infinite Love, because they have loved,' he concluded.

'But surely it is enough, then, just to love,' I said. 'It hardly matters to us whether we know God or not.'

'That is very far from the truth! You will discover as time goes by that God who loves us has only one great passion — he longs to reveal himself to the one he loves. And the one who is loved by God also has only one desire — he longs to know the name and the face of his Love. That mutual knowledge is important, for, in it, it is possible for the Lover and the loved one to receive each other and to give themselves to each other.'

I left the Sage without a further word. I was happy and at peace and went away knowing that, for me, God had today become no longer something, but *Someone*.

16

It was a beautiful moment. The realisation that I was looking for Someone who was God made me happy, but at the same time I was strangely troubled by it.

I felt unable at that moment to follow the flight of my heart. I knew that I had been set free, but I could only stumble and grope my way forward on the path that lay before me.

All around me, life remained the same. Nothing had changed. The real world of my work and my private life was still there. The sun was not shining in that world and it was not so attractive as my dream — for I was already wondering whether it may have been no more than a beautiful dream.

The people all around me seemed to be very distant, despite their physical proximity. I felt that their thoughts were very far from mine and their vision was very different from the one I had recently been given. So I could not share either my joy or my hopes and fears with anyone. And in any case, even if I had been able to express my feelings, I would hardly have dared to. They would, I felt sure, have laughed at me.

Again and again it seemed to me that the sun was not shedding its rays in the world of my everyday experience. It was only much later that I realised that this was because the light was within me and it would only shine on the way when my heart caught fire. In the meantime, I continued to feel alone.

But what I had discovered during that last session with the Sage brought about a positive change in my life. I went out less frequently and, instead of trying to fill my room with the noise of the television, radio or recorded music, I sought silence.

That was a very important change. Perhaps as a result of it, I also tried very hard to look at the people I met not with indifference or hostility, as I so often had in the past, but with sympathy and love. I also trained myself to listen to them, even when what they were saying seemed trivial.

Sometimes it seemed to me that I was committing myself to the service of others, very nearly without wanting to. It was as though a power deep within me had been set free and made available and was driving me to serve others in often very small ways. Could it have been the Breath?

I had to admit it — I could barely recognise myself any more, I had changed so much. I was firmer and much more decisive and at the same time I also felt weaker and more insignificant. I knew that I could never live and love as I felt driven to, just on my own.

I needed Someone. That Someone was not the God of my past, but the God of my Friend the Sage, God-Love. I still did not know that true God, certainly, but I surprised myself by the many times that I found myself praying to him. At least, I believe I was praying at those times! I was still uncertain about what prayer really was.

It was at this time that I received this letter from the Sage:
'First of all, my son, I have to say how sorry I am for talking too much when we were last together. But patience! There must always be a long interval between sowing and reaping. It would be foolish to harvest corn that is still growing.

'Forgive me! But I have suffered from the same hunger and thirst as yourself and, like you, I have also discovered what was hidden deep in my heart beneath that hunger and thirst — a longing to love and even more to be loved.

'I too have searched for God and have found him coming to meet us in Jesus Christ. I have believed in him. I have believed in his Word. I now know that I have always been loved — long before I began my search. "In this is love, not that we loved God, but that he loved us . . ." And the more I discover of the depths of his Love, the more I love him.

'It is true to say that the one who loves and is loved cannot prevent himself from making the one he loves known to others. That is why I spoke to you — perhaps too much.

'But the sound of my voice should not make the whisper of his Word inaudible! I can only put you on the way leading to an encounter between hearts. It is he who will declare his love to you.

'So go out to meet him who is coming to meet you!

'Anyone who claims that it is possible to live without Life and love without Love is very mistaken!

'For the believer, prayer is life. To forget to pray is to forget how to live.

'It is right that we should be in control of our earth and increase that control every day, using all our skills. That is what God wants — he has put us in charge of his creation. But many people's lives are sterile because they think they can do that without God. They forget that it is not the ship's sails that make the wind blow. They spend more time designing magnificent ships, building them and repairing them than exposing themselves to the wind that makes them sail over the ocean.

'They think they can do without God altogether. Each one thinks that he or she is God and tries to increase in stature by exploiting others. But we shall only be able to live truly and justice and peace will only reign in the world when all people together are able to call the one God "our Father" and say to him: "You are our Life and our Love. We are your sons and daughters and each other's brothers and sisters".

'And that, my son, is why I asked you to pray!

Praying is going forward to meet our Father, God-Love.

Prayer is saying to God:

'Source, give me living water
flowing between the banks of my everyday life.
Without you I would become stagnant water and die.

Sun, give me light
shining on my way today and tomorrow.
Without you I would live in darkness and be lost.

Wind, fill my sails
— they are hoisted to receive you.
Without you I would never leave the harbour.

Breeze, I am waiting for your breath
to carry me on my flight.
Without you, I would be a bird with polluted
feathers.

63

Artist,   touch me with your bow
and draw music from my strings and my wood.
Without you I would remain for ever silent in my
                                   case.

God,   great Artist, I am here, receptive
as a violin held in your loving arms,
waiting for you to play me.
I offer myself to you as your bride
– embrace me in your Love
and our child will be
music that will make the world sing with joy.'

The Sage's letter ended with these simple words:

'Yes, you must pray, for prayer is
going out to meet God who is coming to meet us,
knowing that he is our Life and our Love,
being totally recollected
and offering ourselves totally
to be loved even before we love others.'

64

17

I prayed. Yes, this time I really prayed. And as I prayed, I was accompanied by a feeling of astonishment.

My parents, friends and acquaintances did not even suspect this great change that had taken place in me. I would not have dared to tell them! Not because I was ashamed, but because I feared they might smile or say something that would spoil the growth of this beautiful flower in me.

When I prayed, it was not just with words. I prayed with the whole of my being, putting myself in the presence of the one who was, I knew, infinitely present in the darkness. And I found that I could let myself be loved more easily in silence.

I felt that prayer was essentially silence. My friend assured me later, when I spoke to him about it, that this was so.

It also did not take me long to understand, in this first real experience of prayer, that it was wrong to try to get into favour with God — he was not the omnipotent God of my past!

My prayer did not consist of asking either for favours or for things. All that I sought was the power to live and to love.

But that was not easy! My heart was restless and burning with desires of every kind. It was, it seemed to me, like a market place full of noise and confusion.

Yet this did not trouble me. My heart resembled the world outside, where I met my friends and acquaintances, smiled at them and spoke to them, listened to their problems and carried their burdens for a little way — on my way to my Source.

Much later I learned that Jesus had said:

'Whoever drinks
of the water that I shall give him
will never thirst.

**The water that I shall give him
will become in him
a spring of water
welling up to eternal life.'**

I was sure that Life was to be found there. But it was not easy!

It was not easy because of the habits I had acquired in the past and because many of my questions remained unanswered.

Those questions had become more urgent now and they got in my way more. I still very much needed the Sage to enlighten me and I knew I would continue to need him for a long time to come.

On my first visit to him after receiving his letter, I asked him: 'You told me once that I should expect everything from God. But if I wait for him to give me everything, what is there left for me to do?'

'Everything is left for you to do!' was his immediate reply.

**'Not even the greatest artist can play on broken strings.
The wind cannot drive forward a ship with torn sails/
The glacier cannot give birth to a mighty river
    if its bed is full of rubbish.
And God-Love can do nothing
if we do not work in freedom to fashion our own lives
and to build up the world for our brothers and sisters.**

'We are free to do nothing or to do everything we can,' he continued, 'And at the same time we have to expect everything from Love. Without that Love, nothing is possible and nothing will live and flourish.'

'But we often do things so badly. Our work is sometimes atrocious. Why does God let us make so many terrible mistakes?'

'Because he cannot prevent us,' the Sage replied.

'But he can do anything!'

'He can do everything except take away our freedom.'

I did not want to understand that. I suddenly recalled all the mistakes I had made in the past because of that freedom. I thought of the times others had hurt me or treated me unjustly — because of that freedom. I thought of the enormity of human suffering at every level in the world — sickness, hunger, injustice, war, the list was endless. And God was unmoved by all that suffering! How could I believe in such a God?

All that certainty that had built up inside me suddenly began to shake on its foundations and the whole structure seemed about to collapse. I thought I had overcome all doubt, but clearly I had not. It was still very much alive.

I still doubted Love and that filled me with alarm.

'Why has God given us freedom if it brings suffering and death?' I was so angry I was almost shouting.

'Because he loves us,' the Sage replied calmly.

'But letting those you love languish in prison, be tortured, die of hunger, kill each other and be killed — that cannot be love!'

My anger grew as I thought of all the unheard prayers of those who for centuries had cried out in vain to God for themselves or for their loved ones.

I wanted God to hear and answer me. For my own sake and for others. I had to get to the root of my doubt and destroy it once and for all time. I could not continue to live with it in my heart.

'Calm down, my dear boy,' the Sage said.

'Would a mother really be loving her baby
    if she refused to give birth to it
    because the world is an evil place?
Would she really be loving her child
    if she refused to let her learn to walk
    because the world is a dangerous place
    and she might be hurt?
Would she really be loving her adolescent son
    if she locked him indoors
    because he had not learned how to live and love?'

We were both silent. I had nothing to say. But I sensed that my inner struggle would be renewed when I was alone in my own room again.

While I was still with the Sage, however, I had the unpleasant impression that it would be useless to argue with him. I was in a rebellious state of mind, but I knew that I agreed with him in the depths of my heart.

I think what I found so disarming about my Friend was his calm. I felt sure he did not want to convince me of the truth of what he was saying in order to win an argument. He only wanted to make me understand because he wanted to help me.

I believe that was why I was convinced he must be right.

He began speaking again.

'A mother who really loves her child is able — precisely because of that love — to expose her to the risk of falling, hurting herself and even being killed, rather than deprive her of her freedom to live. And she knows in advance that her child is bound to suffer.

'She may be afraid to take that risk and refuse to let herself be separated from her child. She may go on carrying her and protecting her from danger. But if she does, she will put to death in her the adult that she should become.'

'But if her child hurts herself,' I said, no longer angry now after what the Sage had just said, 'will she leave her unattended, treating her as though she were already adult?'

'No, she will not leave her unattended. She will run to her and be as close to her as she can in order to share her suffering.'

'But that will not get rid of the pain.'

'Of course not! But if the child lets herself be loved, she will be strengthened and be able to bear the pain. When someone is touched by real love, that love makes an energy that has so far remained hidden spring up inside that person.'

He paused for a moment, then went on:

'Loving is recreating the other person. And when God loves us, he gives us new life, which is eternal life. But we are free! We are free to reject that love or to be open to receive it.

'Because God is love, he was bound to create us free and, because he is our Father, he was bound to create us responsible — individually for ourselves and each other and collectively for humanity and the universe. We have grown to adulthood and our power over the world and human life has also grown.'

'But we are still very weak!' I said.

'We are proud of our freedom and forget that it comes from God, but when we misuse it we ask him to put our mistakes right. But, because he does not intervene in a purely human way, we cease to believe in him and in his love. If he were to intervene by taking over control of our world from us, he would not be respecting our freedom and would therefore not be loving us.

'But he has sent his Son as God-man to us to reveal his infinite Love. So in Jesus, God is not standing at a distance while he watches us making mistakes that cause him great suffering. Jesus is very close to us, but the only power he has is that of saving self-giving Love.

'Jesus does not leave us alone with our burden of suffering. He bears it with his own and, in giving his life for us, he gives us back our own, set free. He recreates us and gives us new life.

'You must be patient, my son! It may take you a long time to understand the mystery of Love and be able to love truly. I am not surprised by your anger and frustration, because I have experienced those feelings too. I have often felt like cursing God in his terrifying silence and his beautiful but tragic gift of freedom that has so often made our world a battlefield!

'But I know that, if we were not free, we would not be human and able to love. So I accept the wonderful danger of living and loving.'

The Sage sat in quiet recollection for some time after he had finished speaking. When he spoke again, it was to pray aloud to God.

Lord, you could have made us trees in a forest or sheep in a flock.

You could have made us puppets dancing while you pulled the strings.

But you created us human, responsible and free —
sons and daughters free to love you, sisters and brothers free to love each other.
We thank you for that freedom, Lord!

Lord, you could have offered us a finished world —
its roads constructed, its rivers bridged, its cities built
and its factories full of docile workers producing perfect
goods.
But you created us human, responsible and free
and we have the task of building up this world.
We thank you for that freedom, Lord!

Lord, you could have arranged our marriages and given us
our families.
By imposing your will on us, you could have kept us
together in permanent wedlock, peace and love.
You could have counted our kisses, regulated our embraces
and controlled our friendships.
But you created us human, responsible and free —
not dolls made of human flesh to be held in your arms,
but loved human children, richly endowed with life
and free to love you or to refuse your love.
We thank you for that freedom, Lord!

But, Lord, sometimes we behave badly and forget you,
our Father.
We destroy what you have created for us in our fragile
world and take for ourselves what you gave to others.
We struggle for power and exploit, injure and kill one
another.

Lord, you could have ceased to trust and love us and have
withdrawn the power you gave us.
You could then have taken our place and made a heaven
on earth.
But you wanted us to remain human, responsible and
free!

So Lord, you sent us your Son, who was human, responsible
and free,
to love us and save us without taking back our freedom.

And, Lord Jesus, you could have changed stones into
    bread and fed those among us who are dying of hunger.
You could have exerted your power and made us obey you.
    But you wanted us to remain human, responsible and
    free!

Lord Jesus, you could have conquered your enemies and
    given us peace.
You could then have reached your Father's heaven by a
    different way, not the way of the cross.
    We would then have remained human and responsible,
    but we would have remained alone
    with our sins and our guilt,
    all that is left of love when it fails.

But, Lord Jesus, you embraced our sins and our guilt
    when you embraced the dead wood of the cross
    and gave the tree new life and it bore new fruit.
    That fruit is saving Love that sets us free.

Lord, I love you, because you love me and want me to
    be free.
I love you, because you risked your glory for my freedom.
I love you, because you were omnipotent,
    but came to us without power,
    except for the power of Love.

Lord, I love you, because the terrible freedom that causes
    such suffering
is also the wonderful freedom that enables us to choose
    love.

So, when we fall under the cross that we carry every day
    or are angry about the cross borne by our fellow-men
    and curse God or simply sit with our eyes and ears closed,
give us the strength to stand up and go on our way again,
    knowing that you will only help us to carry our cross
    if we carry it ourselves as you carried yours.'

Part II
The Face of Love

18

How dangerous the light can be! This was something that I was learning from my own painful experience. At night-time the dirt and untidiness in a room can remain unseen, but as soon as the morning sun shines through the windows, the dust and disorder are at once revealed.

I did not want the Sage to visit the room of my heart. It was cluttered with the rubbish of everything that I had ever thought, imagined, dreamed and all I had experienced, looked for and tried and failed to do. To this had been added all my recent attempts to love or at least what I called attempts to love.

Some of the memories that filled my poor and suffering heart were positive and good, of course, but very many of them were sad, ugly and destructive. And all of them were very persistent. They were like the old and often damaged and valueless objects that are kept, heaven knows why, piled up in the junk-room or the attic.

I wanted so much to get rid of them now. But how difficult it was! Unable to clear the rubbish out of my heart, the only thing I could think of doing was to talk about it. The need to talk — and above all, I realised, to talk to the Sage — became urgent and I felt that this would perhaps set me free. But I did not want to let him see the shameful contents of my heart. What would he think of me? Would I lose his friendship that I valued so much?

But talking to him about the dreams and fantasies that had accumulated in my heart proved much easier than I had thought. I had forgotten how well he listened — without interrupting, but with a total attentiveness that was almost tangible.

So I went on to tell him about the mistakes I had made in the past, especially those wrong and harmful attempts to love that had hurt me so much and, I felt, must have injured others even more. But bringing all these hidden memories out into the open was unimaginably painful!

So painful in fact, that I was conscious of keeping my head bowed and of speaking more and more slowly and hesitantly. From time to time I raised my head and looked cautiously at the Sage's face, expecting to see criticism, reproval or condemnation in his eyes. But no — I always encountered warmth and reassurance. My shameful confession had not diminished his love for me in any way.

When I had finished speaking, he waited — in case I wanted to add to what I had already said — and then murmured: 'How you must have suffered.'

'If only I had known you a long time ago,' I said.

He made no reply to this, but simply said: 'Some people have learned from their earliest childhood how to love because they have always lived in a loving environment, so they are able to avoid hurting themselves and others.

'But not all trees are lucky enough to grow in entirely good soil. Most trees have their roots in soil that is partly fertile and partly stony and unyielding, so that they have to feel their way in the dark until they find the nourishment they are seeking to make them bear fruit.

'We are very similar and it is not bad for us to have to make our way groping in the dark. If everything comes to us easily and without a struggle, we are likely to fall in the first little wind.

'If we are faithful in our search for Life, that Life will come to meet us on the wings of Love and find us. After all, Love is not just 'something', but Someone who is always present with us.'

I felt that he had put me at my ease, but he had not completely reassured me. So I went on insistently, almost against my will:

'But I cannot get rid of all the mistakes I have made. I go on carrying them around with me like a great burden on my back and they slow me down.

'I often try very hard to forget them, but I find it impossible to overcome the harm I have done to myself and to

76

other people. Will I ever be able to put right the damage to my heart and body and those of others?'

'It is not a question of forgetting!' the Sage exclaimed with a sharpness that surprised me.

'What should I do then?' I asked at once.

'You should give everything!'

'Give everything? But how do I do that?'

'First of all by not burying or concealing from yourself any wrong action you have committed in the past. You must keep it in the light and continue to look straight at it. The life that you may think you have buried continues to live in you and, if you fail to acknowledge its presence or to recognise it, it will take its revenge.

'But do not be afraid to relive the events that have perhaps scarred you and others because of you in the past. Do not be afraid to call bad what is bad, to expose the wounds that you have inflicted on yourself and on others. You must give everything and you can only give what you are holding in your own hands.'

'But to whom should I give everything?' I asked.

'Give it to the one who came to bear our burden — Jesus Christ.'

'And what can he do with it?'

'He can treat it like dead, useless wood — throw it on the fire. Then it will become warmth and light for those gathered around the hearth.

'Give all your past mistakes and all your sufferings to Jesus Christ, my son, and his Love will burn them all and Life will be given back to you.'

I could not keep a note of scornful disbelief from my voice: 'But that is altogether too simple!'

'No, it is not simple! It is very difficult! It is difficult to believe that Love is more powerful than our mistakes. But I assure you that it is the way we are really set free.'

Set free from the mistakes of my past! I resolved to try that way. But at once I thought: Tomorrow! How would I react tomorrow? My old hunger and thirst would return, as strong and as confused as ever. What would I be able to do to satisfy them tomorrow?

Secretly I felt a great resentment — not for the first time — against the Sage for opening my eyes to my own mistakes

77

and insisting that I should not bury them. But at the same time, even though I knew I was being carried along by a mysterious force that came from outside myself and beyond me and was tossing me about like a straw in the wind, I also knew that I would tomorrow be as I was today.

What did it matter, then, if I could not catch a glimpse of the beauty of love, since I could not incorporate it into my life?

'But why is it so very difficult to love?' I asked.

'Because loving is bringing together and uniting,' he replied without a moment's hesitation, 'in a world that has been broken into thousands of fragments. Our task is to put the human pieces of the gigantic jigsaw puzzle of the world together.

'It is a difficult task, but a wonderful one. Two forces are at work in it — on the one hand, the power of division, selfishness and pride and, on the other, the power of unity. The power of unity is the power of love. Division and selfishness end in death, but love ends in life. And the struggle between them takes place in your heart and my heart and in the heart of every human being. Your life has positive value if it projects the power of unity and love into the world.

World, our world,
    from the very beginning
    we have been destined to marry you
    at the eternal wedding feast!
    You grow in the womb
    and then, made but unmade,
    in fragments and incomplete,
    you are given to us
    for us to remake and complete you.

The virgin soil has to be cleared, broken and prepared
    before it can be made fertile
    by the river flowing through it
    and the rain falling on it.
The seed has to be sown in drills made by man
    before the wheat can grow in the fields

The green ears of wheat have to be caressed by the breeze
and married to the bronzing rays of the sun
before the harvest can be gathered.
The corn has to be ground and mixed with yeast
and the dough has to be married to the heat of the oven
before the bread can be baked and eaten.

The body and heart of each of us have to be united
before we can be responsible for ourselves and others.
The human spirit has to be married to matter
before that matter can be made to serve life.
We have to bring stone and wood together
before we can build our own home
We have to unite metal, sand and fire
before we can build a bridge
to unite the two banks of a river
and cross to the other side.

We have to stretch out a hand to others
before real friendship can exist
We have to lead the struggle for justice on to love
before freedom can begin to live.
Man has to marry woman in love
before Joy can be born
and the child of that Joy.

God has to be three
and those three have to be one
before Love can live in the Holy Trinity.
God has to become and be Man
before we can become divine as God's children.
And we have to be free,
made fruitful by the Spirit
and gathered together in the Church
before we can become one living Body.

United, one universe, humanity and God
married in Love,
we can make heaven in eternity.

World, our world,
    you grow in the womb
    and then, made but unmade,
    in fragments and incomplete,
    despite all divisions, struggles and defeats,
    you are moving towards unity,
    the oneness for which you were made.

For, on that great day in the history of the world,
    Jesus was nailed to the immense cross
    of the world
    and in the depths of his heart
    he recreated the world
    and made it new.

And, although I am weak and insignificant
    in that immense history,
    I am also an essential member
    of that great living Body
    and I offer myself with the world
    to the task of Love.'

The Sage ceased to meditate aloud and he seemed to derive refreshment from his silence. I was reminded of orators who take a drink of cool water after having burnt their lips on the fire of their speech.

I got up to leave without a word. I knew the Sage accepted my going in this way. He simply smiled and that, I knew, meant: 'I will look forward to seeing you again soon.'

19

I found it very difficult to go to sleep that night. I lay awake haunted by the memories of the past that the Sage had suggested I should not keep buried, but bring confidently into the light. I was, however, not confident, but full of resentment! Above all, I felt very bitter towards my parents for having told me so much and yet so little about love and for having given me such an imperfect example of it. And I also disliked myself because I had until recently been so proud of my successes with girls.

The Sage had suggested that I should confront my past if I really wanted to be set free from it, but previously he had made another suggestion — that I should pray.

Yes, I would follow his earlier suggestion. That might prove easier. Lying awake with my bad memories and thoughts, I spoke to God:

Lord, I offer you my past because you are asking me for it.
I give you the memories that have been hidden in the junk-
room of my mind.

Is it true that you put all our rubbish to positive use,
even if it is what is called sin?
Is it true that for you nothing of us is lost,
so long as we give it to you?
Is it true that you make what is dead live again?

Lord, open my heart!
Open my hands
that are now so tightly closed!

I said these words — and many others as well — again and again, but I only encountered the painful silence of God.

On my next visit to the Sage, I told him: 'When I listen to you, I cannot help believing what you say is true. But when I listen to my own heart, and even more when I listen to my own body, I can only secretly consent to their claims. There seems to be a conflict between the two voices. Which is right?'

'Both are right,' he replied. 'Let me explain:

'There are not two voices, but only one.
There are not two lives, but only one
   and there is only one Energy at the centre of that one life.

That Energy is the Power of unity —
   "the Spirit of God moving over the face of the waters".

Countless millennia ago, that mysterious Energy
   brought scattered elements of organic matter together
   so that the first cell would live.

Today, that same mysterious Energy
   moves, sings and calls
   in the flesh of the universe
   so that it will continue to live and grow.

That mysterious Energy makes the root that loves the soil,
                     the ear of wheat that loves the sun,
   the bird that loves the ocean
   and crosses it each year to make its nest,
   and the male and the female of every species
   that love, seek out and are united to each other.

There is not a multiplicity of lives, but only one.

Many millennia ago, that same mysterious Energy
      made one creature walk upright and with raised head,
   opened his arms so that he could fashion the earth,
   made his body burn with longing for another human
                                                    body,

82

enabled him to think and to know himself and his
                                    brothers and sisters,
and made his heart long for the light and for life.

It is also that same mysterious Energy,
    coming from the depths of time
    and the act of creating the universe and countless human
                                                    beings,
        that is rising up in you today
        like an underground stream,
        feeling its way towards the sea

and causing those desires that trouble you so deeply
            with their urgent power that cannot be satisfied,
    those desires for air, water, sun and earth,
    that longing to live and grow,
    that longing for knowledge
    and above all that longing in your heart
    for the heart of a woman,
    and in your body for her body —
    that longing for oneness.

There is not a multiplicity of lives, but only one
                    and its source is the Love of God
    who has created and continues to create
    the universe, this world and humankind.

God said: "I am the Life" and those words are true.'

I had a sudden conviction that I was at the crossroads of
that Life. I knew that it was not my life and that it did not
belong to me, but that it had come to me from afar. I knew
too that it had always filled me as it had always filled all the
others. And I was, I saw now with great clarity, at one with
them and was sharing with them the same experience of a
great Adventure.

But I also recognised that I was afraid of that mysterious
Energy of which the Sage had spoken. It was blowing like a
great wind and in the right direction, but I was a bad sailor
and my sails were wrongly set. I was still heading for the reefs!

I continued to think about that Life and my own failed

life, but was soon compelled to listen to the Sage as he continued with his meditation in a firm and resonant voice:

'Your children must know this life is beautiful!

They must know before longing is aroused in them,
              when life is flowing peacefully in their veins,
that this life that comes from afar
    was born in them from the longing of their parents
    when bodies were enlaced and hearts consented.

Your children must know this life is beautiful!

They must know when the sap is rising secretly within them
                  and the buds are breaking open,
and they are searching anxiously for the cause of this
      torment and are looking in the loneliness of their hearts
for a heart that is not the heart of their father or mother.

Your children must know this life is beautiful!

They must know when their bodies are bleeding as their
                          life is flowing away,
and they are asking why and for whom their life is
                  expended without giving life in return
and when they are feverishly making a voyage of discovery
          and have set foot on the island of their own body
    and have tried to gather the fruit that is growing there
    and are dreaming of other islands and other treasures.

Your children must know this life is beautiful!

They must know when their thoughts are suddenly filled
              with the light of a face and the shape of a body
and when their innocent fingers suddenly tremble
      and cannot be sure whether it is an illusion.

Your children must know this life is beautiful!

They must know when longing is aroused in them
              like a fire lit after the dark cold night
and they are made uneasy because the little flames
                      that give warmth and light

84

can blaze into a configuration
and destroy everything.

But your children must know this life is beautiful!'

The Sage came towards me and surprised me by embracing me. Then he held me at arms' length and looked steadily at me.

'Your children must know this life is beautiful,' he repeated and added: 'And you will tell them, about the beauty of this life! They feel their way forward, hurting themselves and each other. They are searching for love, but they kill it in the belief that they have found it.

'Your children must know this life is beautiful!

They must know that it is a river
flowing from the depths of time
and trying to flow through their bodies
that have become too small to contain it.

They must know that it is the Breath of Love
coming from infinity, making their hearts beat
and making them look for another heart
that will beat in time with their own.

They must know above all that what can be heard
in the mystery of the hunger and thirst
that makes them suffer so much
in their bodies and hearts
is the small voice of God.

And they must know what that voice tells them:
"I have made you in my image and likeness
and I love you with all my heart.
So do not suppress that longing,
even if it makes you afraid.
Do not suppress my voice
but listen to it in your longing.

Do not be afraid!
Even in the storm of your desires,
I am calling you.

I am on board with you
and I will help you."'

The Sage had let go of me during his meditation. His eyes
were closed now and I knew he had closed them in order to
see God more clearly. What is more, he could see with his
eyes closed what I could not yet see.

Surely contemplation is no more than seeing as he was
able to see! He was contemplative because he was able to
see beyond and into the heart of the things, events and
people of his everyday life. He looked at the earth and saw
the roots of the tree growing in it. He looked at the tree and
saw the sap rising in it and the flowers and the seed that it
would later bear. He looked beyond and into the heart of
our human life and saw the mystery of Love calling on us to
bear fruit that would last.

Yes, I knew the Sage could see beyond and into the heart,
while I was still only able to see the surface of things, events
and people. I was still very incomplete, a child just beginning
to discover a little of the mysterious world that was waiting
for me.

The Sage spoke again, this time in a very low voice:

'How beautiful it is when a young person becomes open
                        to love
  and feels his way forward in the darkness!
How beautiful it is when two young people look at each
                         other
  come close to each other and touch each other
  and tentatively get to know one another,
  called to be united and longing for a child!
Why do we only see their mistakes
  and the times they fall and hurt themselves?
Why do we only smile at them or condemn them,
  when we should admire and help them on their way?'

The Sage opened his eyes and looked at me.
'When you have fully understood that the infinite beauty
of God himself shines in love because it is the living reflection

of himself in us, then you will be able to tell your children: "Your search is wonderful!"

'You will no longer need to say: "That is wrong! It is forbidden!" You will simply tell them: "Love is a great Adventure. It is very difficult, but it is very beautiful".'

20

Yes, the Adventure of Love was very beautiful, but I found it difficult to reflect about the beauty of Love and preferred to think about my own longings and my attempts to satisfy them.

I had come to recognise that I was unconsciously seeking something that lay beyond the hunger and thirst of my body. Only recently I had been powerfully attracted to a girl in my circle of friends. Previously I would have let myself be dominated by my longing for her. But now I listened to the quiet voice of my heart telling me: 'No, that is not what you are looking for.' I was, I now knew, seeking something that would give me more than fleeting satisfaction.

Unconsciously seeking! Yes, I was not yet aware that the longing that I experienced and that sometimes caused me such suffering was really a call from God. He was inviting me to set off, on a way that was much longer than and very different from the paths which I had been following and which led nowhere, in search of that Adventure of Love that was so difficult for me to understand.

Today was for me perhaps the most important of my life. I decided to respond to God's appeal and set off on that long journey.

The Sage knew me very well. He knew I was like a spirited horse that had been kept tethered for too long and he was afraid that, released from the stable, I would bolt.

'It is wonderful to watch a young person set himself free and escape from captivity without knowing where he is going or what he is seeking,' he said. 'He does not know that what he is seeking is the Face of Love. Nor does he know how long the way is to that encounter. It is a very long and hard way, but it is also very beautiful, because it leads to the heart of infinite Love.'

'Show me that way,' I said, 'and I will follow it.'

'You will have to be a man first, my son!'

'But I am a man!' I replied sharply. His words had hurt me!

'No, you are not yet a man! The man who is being born in you is not yet complete.'

'What should I do, then, to become complete?'

'The life you receive from others, from the world and from God must become your life. An animal receives its life from others too, but, unlike us, it has no share in its own creation. Everything is programmed for it and it is guided by its instincts.

'Your parents made you a little child, but you have gradually to make yourself a man. It is your task to develop all the vital forces in yourself, give them direction, unify them and integrate them. A river has its life from its source and its tributaries. Without that life-giving water, it dies. The more fully you possess and are in control of your own life, the more fully you will be a man. And then you will be able to pronounce the word "I" and say "*I* think, *I* speak, *I* act" in freedom and "*I* am coming to you, my love whom *I* love."

'But unfortunately very few people fully possess or are fully in control of their own lives. Some keep their life close to themselves, imprisoned. Their life frightens them or they despise it. They treat it like water in a disused well — the very opposite of living water.

'For others it really is living water. But they let if flow between their fingers and it is lost.

'Then there are those people who want to give the life that is in them its "freedom". They open all their doors to their body, their spirit and their heart and say: "Gather all the fruit you can find in the world. Take everything you want when you want it!"

'Poor people! They fondly believe they are free, but in fact they are dependent. They run after life, but it is always eluding them and they become exhausted and dispirited. The river of their life has no bed and no banks. They also have no control over it — it has no dam, no sluice-gate and no weir. It soon becomes a dried up, stony track.'

The Sage paused, then asked: 'Who can live without life?

Who can love if he has nothing to give? Who can sing about love if everyone in the choir is singing his own song in his own time without a score and without a choir-leader?

'If you really want to learn how to love, you must be a man. You must possess yourself and be in control of your own life.

Love is not being dazzled by the beauty of a face
    that suddenly appears before you in the light of day.
True beauty is a reflection of the human soul
    and that is not found without a painful search.

Love is not the fascination of a lively and captivating wit
    that is expressed in words that are aimed to please.
Intelligence can sparkle with a thousand gems —
    without being made of diamond — hidden in the loved
                                 one's heart.

Love is not an emotional response to a heart
    that seems to beat more for you than for others.
A heart can always beat for another
    and leave you suffering with your love still alive.

Love is not a longing to seize and hold an object
    that you covet — body, spirit or heart.
An object is not what the other is
    and, if that is what you love, you love yourself.

Being dazzled, fascinated, emotionally moved, longing —
    these are necessary and often good,
    but only to help us to love,
    if we really want to love.

The doors and windows are open
    and the wind is blowing through the home
The open sea is calling you.
The small voice of God is inviting you
    to go out of yourself,
    in search of the other
    whom you have chosen to complete your life
    because you love and want to love her.

After all, my son,

loving is wanting the other to be quite free
    and wanting to break that person's chains,
so that she can also freely say: 'I love you'
    without being driven by uncontrolled desires.

Loving is going into the other's secret garden
    through the gate that she has opened for you
    and exploring her paths, flowers and fruit,
so that you can eventually say in astonishment:
    "You are the one I love, the only one."

Loving is wanting the other's good
    with all your heart and strength
    even more than you want your own.
It is doing everything to help the other to grow
    and become the complete person she should be
    and not the one you have imagined in your dreams.

Loving is giving your body and not taking the other's,
    but welcoming it when she offers it to you to share.
It is being recollected and enriching your life
    so that you can offer the one you love
    not only physical kisses and embraces,
    but also your entire life and all that you are
    gathered together in the arms of your whole being.

Loving is offering yourself to the other
    even when she rejects you for a moment.
It is giving without taking into account
    what the other gives in return,
    paying a high price
    and not asking for change.
It is giving and forgiving
    if the loved one gives to others
    what has been promised to you.

Loving is setting the table
    and serving the meal for the other
    and knowing you cannot do without the one
    who supplies and prepares the food
    and shares it with you.

91

It is giving and receiving
   for, without the food she brings to the feast,
   you can only serve dry bread and water.

Loving is trusting the other and believing in her,
   her hidden strength and her inner life.
It is clearing the stones to make the way smooth
   and then, after a calm and reasonable decision,
   setting off on a pilgrimage together
   that will go on for ever.

Loving is accepting suffering and dying to yourself
   in order to live and let the other live,
It is forgetting yourself and enduring the pain,
   since no one can cease to live for himself
   unless something suffers and dies within him.

Loving is above all being open to infinite Love
   and letting yourself be loved by that Love.
It is the supreme Adventure of letting God love
   both you and the one you have freely decided to love.'

If that is loving, I wondered, deeply discouraged, at the
end of the Sage's long meditation, how shall I ever suceed
at it? Surely it would be more sensible never to set foot on
the mountain slope, but just to gaze up at the summit from
the safety of the valley!

But, despite all that the Sage had told me, I had not yet
begun to understand that loving was not a point of departure,
but a goal to be reached after a lifetime of following a long
and difficult path! I still wanted to achieve everything at
once! I still had to learn to walk slowly and carefully up
the steep path to the summit.

21

After leaving the Sage, I thought about what loving had been for me in the past and came to the conclusion that it had above all been a question of emotion. The value of any experience I had had of loving depended on the intensity of the feeling and the violence of the desires associated with it.

If the fire that a girl had lighted in me had raged for a long time, then I had loved her more intensely. If, on the other hand, that fire had only flickered and had gone out very soon, then my love for that girl had been less intense.

I had never bothered myself about the ashes, even when they were still glowing in the heart of the girl I had left. It surprised me that the fire could still be burning fiercely in her heart when I was glowing in the heat of another fire. Her unhappiness did not trouble me at all. I was completely unaware of it.

I had also divided my experiences into two groups. Some had been just for my enjoyment, but others, I liked to think, were 'serious' love affairs. Above all, however, I had reassured myself again and again that love did not last. How foolish, I told myself, to expect it to last and to want to commit oneself permanently, because loving obeyed the law of the fire that consumed everything it touched!

Yet all the same I secretly hoped that one day I would encounter a love that was different. A very odd couple I had once known had loved each other in a way that was obvious to all who met them and the old man had continued to love his wife beyond her death. With their example in mind, I continued to wait and hope . . .

But reflecting about my attitude towards loving in the past brought a very disturbing truth to light. I had thought that I had loved those girls, but in fact I had only been loving myself. This revelation shattered me, but I knew it was true.

I had loved myself and only myself! I had loved myself so much that I was incapable of loving others. I had only made use of those unfortunate girls in order to secure a little pleasure or happiness for myself. None of my loving had been 'serious'. It had all been for my own enjoyment.

I had loved girls as I had loved smoking. That longing for a cigarette could only be satisfied by taking one out of the packet, lighting it, inhaling the smoke and throwing the half-smoked butt away, until the next cigarette was put between one's lips. I had done exactly the same with girls.

At the same time, I had wanted to be loved. I had told one girl after another — I knew now without much sincerity or conviction — that I loved her because I wanted her to reply: 'I love you'. If she said this with apparent sincerity, I seized hold of it avidly. How it pleased me to be loved!

I had been alone and I had been looking for someone to end my solitude. I had been wanting to talk and I had been looking for someone to listen to me. I was at the centre of all those experiences of loving!

My body had been calling out for pleasure and I had spent hours contriving to make use of another body that would satisfy my need for tender caresses. If that other body was also longing for the same physical pleasure, my happiness would know no bounds!

Yes, I would no longer conceal from myself the fact that I had only loved myself in the past and that I still loved myself. My experiences of loving had been no more than conquests with the aim of satisfying myself and possessing something I desired. That was so even when the one who shared my experience also desired what I desired and longed for me as much as I longed for her, so that two selfish quests came together and joined for a while before parting.

And that was what I called 'loving' and sometimes even believed was loving!

How could I have gone so terribly astray? For I had no doubt that I had been following the wrong road for a long time. It was very clear to me now that I had to change direction. What was required was nothing less than a complete change of heart — a radical conversion.

I knew that my longings were not unhealthy or wrong and that I had no need to be ashamed of them. That was something I had learned from the Sage. At the same time, however, I also knew that they were wild and uncontrolled. They were like untrained steeds running around the fields of my life. They were more in control of me than I was of them and my attempts to hold them and manage them only ended in my becoming exhausted and discouraged. But I had to control them, I knew, if they were to become reliable horses that would take me where I had decided to go.

I told the Sage all this and was encouraged to see his face light up with approval.

'I am so glad you have come to this conclusion,' he said. 'If you let yourself be dominated by your desires and passions, you will remain enslaved. But if you welcome them and at the same time learn to control them, you will be made free and be able to choose freely.

'We are not born free. We have to acquire freedom. Can anyone sincerely say "I love you" if he is forced to love?'

'I will struggle to set myself free,' I exclaimed, 'and to learn how to be in control of myself.'

'Even if you succeed, you will only be at the beginning of your struggle! Loving is not just being able to choose what you want to take, but deciding to give what you want to give and to whom you want to give it.

'So you will have to struggle every day to transform your longing so that it takes in the will to give and at the same time the will to receive what the other freely chooses to give you.'

I still could not fully understand what the Sage was saying, so I asked him: 'Where do I find love, then, if I have to make so much effort to love?'

'It is precisely that repeated effort to love that makes love true!' he answered at once.

'But do I have to forget myself completely in that effort? Must I deny myself?'

'Not at all! You must welcome the whole of life and do everything to unify it, enrich it and develop it if you are to give it to others. And giving life to others is not losing it! It is finding it — like a grain of wheat that gives itself to the

95

field. It falls into the earth and dies and bears much fruit.

'You will eventually meet a girl. She will become your field and you will become hers. And the harvest that both of you will yield will be the result of your shared seed and earth.'

'That is a very beautiful idea,' I said, 'but who can ever love as we ought to love?'

'No one,' he replied at once, 'Only God loves perfectly, because he is entirely giving and entirely receiving. His giving is infinite and his receiving is infinite. That is why he is not simply the one who loves more than anyone else, but is Love itself.

'We are not God. We are simply the image of God and our task is gradually to discover that image and set it free. We are like sculptors, working with a piece of rough stone. We have to make the statue that is contained in that stone emerge in all its beauty.

'Great, wonderful and very difficult Adventure of Love,
      you are man's unique and supreme vocation!
If he does not respond, he cannot find eternal happiness,
          since he was conceived from the beginning by God,
in his tender Love, to love and to be loved.

Father, may the Breath of your Love,
    who created and continues to create me
    as a mother makes her child of her own life
    in the secrecy of her womb,
help me to be a little more like you — orientated towards
                                                    others
offering them my life and receiving theirs.'

'What you are saying, then, is: If I am really orientated towards others and love them as God loves them,' I said tentatively, 'I shall become more myself.'

'Yes, that is what I am saying,' he replied. 'And I am also saying that you become yourself if you help others to love, because you are one member of a great body which is growing with you. That is why I have told you again and again to go out in search of other people, to commit yourself to the service of your brothers and sisters. Have you forgotten that already?'

22

I had not forgotten anything! Learning how to love all my brothers and sisters was surely not so very different from learning how to love one girl. The Sage had once again urged me to go out of myself in search of others, but I could not prevent myself from thinking of meeting and loving just one other person. But could two lives ever be perfectly united in love? How very difficult! In fact, almost impossible! And how foolish to try to build up a world of justice and peace when it was almost impossible for even two people to live together in unity!

I put this question to the Sage when I visited him again: 'What can I do to prepare myself to love one girl?'

'Love all your brothers and sisters and then love her!'

'But how can I love her if I do not even know her?'

'An expectant mother does not know the child she is carrying! And what applies to the unborn child also applies to you and your love. The "girl" you do not yet know is preparing herself too, I hope for you, and your present life is already your future life. Do you really believe you will love that unknown girl in a flash, just as soon as you say: "I love you"? No, your love for her is born now and grows day by day, just like a child. And then, when you eventually meet that girl, you will simply offer her the fruits of that mature love.

'So, in the meantime, prepare yourself by thinking of her and live for her by living for all your brothers and sisters.

'And think too of her sisters, all the girls you will meet on your way. You are, after all, on your way through life with them. You are going on a wonderful journey together and you will only make it once.

'On that way you can get to know and love each other and

prepare yourselves and one another for the days ahead of you on the journey. It is so very easy to do the opposite and hurt each other by being uncaring and grasping and playing at love instead of loving.

'So go to her sisters and tell them:

'Lovely girls I meet on my grey days,
    how I need you all on my journey through life!
You can help the man you really desire
    to be born and to grow in me.
Together you can be my mother
    by giving me the life I need.

Lovely girls I meet on my grey days,
    are you conscious of your power?
I see you every day on my daily journey
    and you bring back the memory of springtime,
    of heady music, invitations to the dance,
    the golden fruit of autumn on my parched lips,
    refreshing spring water after the fever of night,
    and the rising sun and its warm rays
    tenderly caressing my heart.
As you pass by, I think of lissom bodies,
    waves and foam and I want so much to be in the sea.

Lovely girls I meet on my grey days,
    you waken me from my winter sleep
    and force me to go out of myself
    — out of my warm and comfortable room
    with its door closed against disorder.
You nimbly loosen my fingers like those of a child
    and open my eyes and turn them away from myself.
You are the daughters of Eve and you draw me irresistibly
    towards a distant and mysterious place elsewhere
    where your treasure is kept inviolate.

Lovely girls I meet on my grey days,
    what is your secret?
    Where are you leading me?
    What are you giving me?

You pick the flowers growing in your meadows
   and offer them to me from afar,
   making me go far from my parents
   and the house where I was born.
Searching for you I have no fear of barbed wire
   and cross the highest fences,
   trample underfoot all my precious ideas,
   and let my firmest decisions fall at the wayside.
My best clothes torn to shreds and muddy,
   I run ahead in the hope of holding you
   and making you lie down in the green corn,
   crushing the wheat that will become bread.

Lovely girls I meet on my grey days,
   what have you done to me?
You know that the weeds have been growing in my wild
                           heart,
   killing the grass, the flowers and vegetables.
I have so often neglected my secret garden!
You know that my pilgrim's scrip is full of dead wood
   and that I have gone astray,
but you have needed the heat of the brazier
   and the light from a flame lit for a moment,
so you have set fire to all my delusions
   and have burnt all my dreams.

Lovely girls I meet on my grey days,
   does anything remain in the hearth with its warmth and
                               light?
A few charred branches perhaps, which will never bear fruit
   and the sharp taste of ashes in our cold mouths.
And you are butterflies living for a few summer afternoons
   and letting yourself be borne so high in the air.
But you have burnt your wings now
   and all that reminds you of me
   is not a song but merely a cry.

Lovely girls I meet on my grey days,
   how much I have needed you on my journey through life!

I have not needed your fire-raising gifts on my summer
evenings,
but the infinite tenderness of your dew on my harsher
mornings.
I have needed your cool spring water to moisten the roots
of my tree,
not your violent storms to tear off its branches.
I have needed the clear light from your eyes
to cast out the shadows that obscure my dawn.

I have needed you to say 'no' to me,
when I have wanted you with all my heart to say 'yes'.
I have needed a 'no' that was not poor, scared and awkward,
not a 'no' with a long face or a look of disgust,
but a 'no' with a smile, as refreshing as a cool breeze,
a 'no' that has made me — deep within myself,
because I am too proud to confess it openly —
respect you for saying 'no',
a 'no' that has convinced me
that love is a flower that is too beautiful
to be torn out of the ground just because I want it
and then thrown aside and trampled underfoot.

O Jesus, my God, you were able to love so well!
I ask you to be with all those lovely girls today,
to go with them on their journey through life
and, when their paths and mine cross,
help them to give me and all other men
what they can give us so well because they are women:
a longing to go out of ourselves instead of remaining
enclosed within ourselves,
a longing to forget ourselves instead of thinking about
ourselves,
a longing to go beyond ourselves instead of remaining
where we are
and a longing to give to others instead of taking from them.

'This is because the girls we men meet on our grey days are
lovely and they can teach us above all how to love.'

23

'But what should I do about that one girl?' I asked the Sage at the end of his meditation. 'You still have not told me how I should love the girl I hope to meet. What should my thoughts about her be? How should I pray for her?'

The Sage remained silent. I could not understand why he did not answer my question. He seemed to be reflecting. He had spoken a great deal about loving others, especially the girls I met on my way through life, but not about loving that one girl I was hoping to meet. But he had urged me to prepare myself now for that meeting.

I gradually became aware of the fact that he was not looking at me, but at an antique cupboard in his room. I had often admired its shape and its beautiful carving, but had never looked at it closely before. He had once told me that it had belonged to his great-grandparents.

The Sage got up and went over to it now. He looked inside it for a moment, then carefully took out a little wooden casket which was also very old and delicately carved. He opened it, took out the papers that it contained and carefully untied the string holding them together. As he looked through them for the one he was seeking, he began to speak.

'I had great trouble too before I found the way. I tried first one path then another, but always encountered insuperable obstacles and . . .' He hesistated again and, when he finished the sentence, he spoke so quietly that I could hardly hear him: 'I often hurt others when I hurt myself! That is why I can understand you and your difficulty and why I would very much like to help you.'

He was silent again for a long time, then he sighed and said: 'When we love badly, we harm one another so much!'

There was another long silence. My overriding feeling was

one of happiness that the Sage had confessed to me that he
had been and perhaps still was weak like myself. It was comforting to learn that he had also had similar persistent and
very painful difficulties! In the past, when I had told him
about my problems or had listened to him speaking so confidently about love, I had often thought, but never dared to
say aloud: 'If only he knew what it is to seek without finding
and to fall again and again, he would not speak in the way
he is speaking now.'

But now, knowing that his experience had been similar
to my own, I felt differently. Everything he said from now
on would take on a different complexion. His words would
really live for me!

In the meantime, he had found the paper he had been
looking for in the casket. He unfolded it and examined it.
I expected him to read aloud what was written on it. To my
surprise, he refolded it and handed it to me.

'Take it!' he said, 'Read it when you get home.'

He paused. I could see that he was very moved.

'I was like you. I was afraid that I would miss the oppor-
tunity with that one girl and so I wrote this at the time to
help me to pray. I want to give it to you. I would like you to
read it and then forget it as quickly as possible and compose
your own meditation for yourself. That is the right way to
do it — I have had the experience and I can provide the
framework for you, who are still uncertain, to fill in.'

Although it was very late, I read what the Sage had written
so long ago as soon as I arrived home.

'My beautiful love as yet unknown
   you are living and breathing
   somewhere far away or perhaps quite close to me,
but I still know nothing
   of the threads that form the fabric of your life
   or the pattern which makes your face distinctive.

My beautiful love as yet unknown,
   I would like you to think of me tonight
   as I am thinking of you —

not in a golden dream that is far from my real self,
but as I really am, a living person
that cannot be invented without distorting the truth.

My beautiful love as yet unknown,
I love you already although your face is hidden.
If I can make myself richer now
I shall be able to enrich you
and I want to learn how to give
rather than always to take.
When you enter my life and I recognise you,
I do not want to take you like a thief.
I want to receive you like a treasure
and let you give yourself to me.

My beautiful love as yet unknown,
will you forgive me in the future?
I hope you will forgive me
when you are curled up beside me
and when your eyes seek out the most distant clouds
in the open sky of my eyes.
I hope you will forgive me,
for knowing too well the gestures of love
because I have learned them from others before you.
I would like to forget them now for your sake!
How lovely it would be if we could seek and find together
the chords that would form the right accompaniment
to the songs of joy and suffering that we shall sing
together!

My beautiful love as yet unknown,
I want to pray for you tonight
because you already exist,
because I already want to be faithful to you
and because you are already having difficulties
and possibly because of me.
I am preparing myself for you
and you are preparing yourself for me.

I hope with all my heart
  that in the future I shall be your sun
  and you will be my source,
  that I will warm you in my rays
  and you will wash me in your water.
Our bodies will be grafted together
  and we shall give to the world
  what it needs most of all —
  the strength of our love
  that it would lack without us.

My beautiful love as yet unknown,
  we have to wait for one another now.
We know how painful it is for lovers
  who do not know each other's faces
  to go on waiting for each other!
But we also know that, although we are still apart,
  our two lives are looking and calling for each other.
And I am also sure that, in the darkness of our longing,
  God's longing and his Light are present.

Our Father who is in heaven
  is looking at us, my love, and loving us.
And he is saying now
  as he has been saying for all eternity:
  "If that is what they really want,
  they will be one in the future."

  That is his dream as our Father
    and that will be our decision as his children.'

Just as the Sage had been deeply moved when he gave me this prayer, so I was moved when I had read it. I found it very beautiful, but at the same time I found it difficult to use it as a basis for my own prayer. I felt that I still did not know him well enough to be able to adapt it to my own situation.

Had he in fact met the 'beautiful love as yet unknown' of his prayer? Had he experienced the love that was expressed in those words? I did not like to ask such questions and decided to respect the mystery of the Sage's love and wait for him to speak about it.

24

I had achieved a victory of a kind, because I now had the courage to talk about the Sage with my friends. That was something that I had found almost impossible to do in the past.

That was, of course, at least partly because we had seldom been serious in each other's company. Whenever we had held discussions, we had never talked about ourselves or our own problems, but only about other people, society or world events. But for the most part our conversation had been frivolous. We had behaved like a group of isolated individuals, each one of us mainly concerned with the task of impressing the others and making them laugh.

One day I tried to tell some of the girls in our circle what I expected of them, what they could offer me and what they were capable of destroying in me. What I said was really no more than what the Sage had discussed with me — that reflected almost exactly what I was feeling and experiencing.

I was taken aback by the violence of their reaction. They defended themselves strenuously and attacked me and all young men.

'You boys think we make every mistake in the world! But that is not true! We are more often than not the victims of your mistakes. You claim every right and we have to be constantly on our guard against you. You certainly want to remain the dominant sex and treat us as though we were just there for your pleasure.'

I tried to defend myself against this attack on my sex, but I did it very badly, partly because there were several of them and I was on my own. Also I did not know how to express my thoughts at the deepest level. They were new to me and I had not fully assimilated them. I even felt a certain shyness.

Was it just a quarrel between young people in late adolescence? It certainly appeared like that on the surface, but at a deeper level, it was much more. The encounter distressed me so much that I had to speak about it to my Friend.

'It is just not possible to express all one's thoughts in a single session, my dear boy! Reality is like a diamond. You do not necessarily forget all its other facets while you are looking at one.

'I think those girls were right.

'I know they have power over young men, but then, so do you young men have power over them. You are made for each other and you are also made *by* each other.

'Mankind would be seriously crippled if one half of it were removed, and everything would go wrong in human society if we failed to recognise that man and woman are equally valuable. They are complementary and they have to be constantly in contact with each other. Neither men nor women can lead sound and healthy lives if both are not equally respected.

'The world that we have shaped for you young people hinders you in many ways rather than helps you. What you are doing now will be, I hope, continued and developed by your children, but the results they achieve will not be balanced or fruitful if yours are not.

'The other day I suggested that you should tell the "lovely girls you met on your grey days" why you needed them on your journey through life. Today I think you ought to listen to what *they* have to tell you:

'**Young man, you have often gone poaching in the wood**
of love
and many girls have let themselves be caught in your arms.
But, when you have boasted to your admiring friends
about your successes,
I have felt sickened, because I am not just game existing
for your pleasure
and you would make me think that you and your friends
are
no more than sad little hunters of girls.

106

I know that chasing the girl you desire gives you a sense
of power
and, when you catch her, that girl who may be forcing
herself to follow you,
you are perhaps, when you take her for yourself,
taking her from someone else.
That other person may be your friend
and he may be dreaming, without even knowing it,
that she is keeping herself for him
like a rose on the rose-tree, not a cut flower.

The wood of my heart is very tender — as delicate as that
of a young tree in springtime.
But you amuse yourself by scratching your name into
my bark
and you do not even know how deeply the knife
penetrates,
making the sap flow from my injured heart.

I have so often had to defend myself against your attacks
and seek refuge in my tower, pulling up the drawbridge.
I am so often afraid of your actions
and your words trouble me even more.
They are able to cross even the deepest moat
and bring you back to me when I do not want you.

You assure me that we have to seek pleasure and enjoyment.
But I am not your plaything and you are not mine
and love is not just a game.
Pleasure may not be a forbidden fruit,
but it is a fruit that has to ripen before it is picked
and we should not steal from other people's orchards,
even if we have an accomplice to let us in by night.

You have often told me that we have to learn how to love,
trying every means at our disposal,
but it is wrong to think of girls as shoes to be tried on
your feet,
one after another — you, laughing with delight,
until you find the right size and shape.

107

Nor is my body a piano keyboard for you to practise your
scales,
so that later you can use another for the recital of your
life.

You tell me that the greatest proof that I can give of my love
is to open for you the doors of my secret rooms.
You are right, of course, I know that!
But, in the meantime, you say again and again you love me
and you want to open them yourself and call for the keys.
But, if you really loved me, you would put out your hand,
tenderly and cautiously, gently seeking my hand
and I would give it to you
and we would go hand in hand
and we would walk together, exchanging thoughts,
talking about you and me, about other people and
about the world.
We would visit the country of our lives together
and patiently strip off the covering that conceals our
two hearts.
We would do this as soon as we came to know each other
and long before we decided to make our two lives one.
Then, once we had declared our intention in the presence
of God and all our friends,
we could finally undress our bodies and become one
and give ourselves Joy
and give them the Child.
How beautiful that would be!

But, in the meantime, you tell me so many things
and you are really wasting your time,
because all the others say the same thing.
It would be better for you to say honestly:
"I am longing for you in my hungry body,
because my heart is thirsty."
I would understand, because I have often longed for you
to come.

Some misty or stormy evenings my doors have been half
open
and I have been waiting and looking out for you
and you would have been able to gather all the honey
you desired
and I would not have had enough love in my heart
to find the strength to send you away.

But you are aware of my dream, my secret and my hard
struggle.
You know that the door of life has been locked in my body
by the fingers of nature and not just by chance.
Although others — not I — have smiled at the idea,
I would like the first to cross the threshold
to be the one my heart has chosen to be wedded to me
for ever,
the only one to break the ground and sow the seed.

The fruit of our love, our child, would eventually ripen.
It would not be long before the fledgling was impelled
to leave the protection of the nest
hidden among the leaves of my tree.

I would like to know, young man: surely you understand me!
But you know as well as I:
I am no stronger than any other girl
and so I need you very much —
as much as you say you need me.

I need to look at you, to be able to admire you
and to be astonished when I discover your hidden riches.
I also need you to look patiently for mine,
for I am often afraid that what I bring to our union
will not be enough to make the man who will learn to
love me rich.
I need you to tell me your thoughts, your feelings and
your plans,
so that I will not be afraid to tell you mine,
because I know that there can be no love between those
who keep secrets from each other!

I need to discover your strength,
  so that I may learn that my gentleness is not weakness,
  but a necessary gift if your harshness is to be tempered.
I need to see you standing and walking on your own
  without the crutches provided by so many willing girls.
I need to prove that you have a heart beating in your breast
  by seeing in your eyes tears that you are not afraid to
                                                  let flow.
I need to see you fight to defend the rights of others,
  so that I can be sure that you will also fight in the future
    for your love and for your own children.

I also need you to look at me, so that you know I really
                                                  exist.
I also need you to look for me and be at my side sometimes,
  so that I may know
  that I am more than someone you seek when you are
                                                  bored.
I also need you to invite me to dance with you from
                                            time to time,
  so that I may know
  that my body is not just a dry branch to be thrown away,
  but a supple and living reed.
I also need to experience the joy of holding your warm
                                            hand in mine
  and the happiness of feeling your arm resting on my
                                            shoulder,
    so that I may know that young men's arms are not
                                            just traps
  set to catch us.

And finally, young men, all of you, I need your *friendship*
  just as you need ours.
But I do not need you all to say to me: "I love you"!
I do not need to hear those insincere words,
  because I may find it difficult to believe that they are true
  when the love I am waiting for comes and says them
                                                  to me.'

For a long time the Sage was so silent that I thought he had finished speaking. But then he added: '*After love, friendship is God's most precious gift to man.* Those who have it are blessed indeed!

'Young men and young women are sent to one another so that, in friendship, they may communicate to each other something of the tenderness and delicacy of God. In that way, they can learn how to love each other.'

I got up to leave the Sage, but it was at that moment that the Child came into the room.

He went behind the Sage, moving so quietly that I was hardly aware of his presence. There was a mischievous look in his eyes as he put his finger to his lips.

He thought the Sage had not seen him, but he was mistaken. My Friend smiled, but did not move as the Child came closer and put his hands over his eyes. My friend pretended for a moment not to know whose hands covered his eyes. Then, as if surprised by his discovery, he exclaimed: 'Why, it is my little angel!'

The little angel laughed, then, standing on tiptoe, he put his head over the Sage's shoulder and kissed him on the cheek. After that, he went out of the room as he had come in, without a word.

The Sage smiled. He was obviously very happy. When he looked at me, I could see that my astonishment pleased him. But he said nothing and neither did I.

When I left the Sage's house, I caught sight of the Child going round the corner of the street.

25

Yes, I was quite sure I would meet that one girl! Whenever I thought of her, I felt lifted up on the wings of a dream into a cloudless heaven. The Adventure of Love is very beautiful, the Sage had assured me, so it would be very beautiful for me with her!

But my dream was very short-lived. The wind of doubt rose very quickly and forced me to return to earth, where I was only conscious of the many obstacles.

When I talked about the Adventure of Love with my friends, they poured scorn on my ideas and, although nothing could shake my conviction that it was beautiful, my doubt as to whether it was possible began to increase.

The Sage never expressed the slightest astonishment at anything I told him and so I had no difficulty in revealing to him what I was thinking, even at the deepest level. Sometimes I even went too far in an attempt to overcome my doubts and said things that must have provoked him. I so much wanted him to convince me!

'Is it reasonable for us young men and women to commit ourselves for the whole of our lives to each other, just because we have fallen in love?' I asked him one day.

'Of course it is, if you are yourselves "reasonable".'

'But if we are not "reasonable"?'

He replied:

'When someone is standing in front of you with his back
$\qquad$ **to the sun,**
$\quad$ **all you can see of his face is a dark outline surrounded**
$\qquad$ **by light.**

In the same way, if you look at yourself only in the light
of your own sensitivity,
all that you will see of yourself is a vague, gilded shadow.
That is not very reasonable.

If someone you do not know knocks on the door of your
heart
and you say: "Come in" without troubling to go out of
yourself and make yourself known to him,
that is not very reasonable.

If the lovers are a prince and a shepherdess
and you say: "There is no difference between them —
the only barrier between them is the one raised by
prejudice,"
that is not very reasonable.

If you spend all your time telling each other: "I love you"
and discovering the taste of each other's lips
and if you have no time left to tell each other
who you are, what you do and what ways you want to
follow,
that is not very reasonable.

If you measure out and weigh exactly how much you will
give each other
and calculate exactly how much it will cost,
there will be no harmony between you because you will
think
that one is giving more and the other is always giving less.
That is not very reasonable.

If you make up your faces and put on costumes
and, to please each other, act the part of the characters
you love,
that is not very reasonable.

If your opinions and your convictions are different
and you want to convert the other to your own view,
that is not very reasonable.

If you say: Let us test the harmony of our bodies
    and check whether they are capable of experiencing
                                                pleasure,
        forgetting that they are interchangeable
        and can deal with pleasures that are sold off cheaply
            without offering love,
                that is not very reasonable.

If your parents and all your real friends tell you:
    We think you are making the wrong choice,
but you say: "What do I care? We love each other!"
    and leave your mooring to set sail together,
        that is not very reasonable.

If you leave the building of your walls unfinished
    and say: "Let us put the roof on the house now,"
        that is not very reasonable.

'But why should I go on adding to the list? You know as
well as I do what is not reasonable. And all lovers know too —
when it concerns others rather than themselves. But when
they are involved personally, they do not want to know!
And that is in itself not reasonable.

'A great love affair which is not a genuine case of loving
often results in a loss of reason. And it is foolish to love
when reason is lost.'

The Sage was smiling, but I did not feel like smiling. I was
irritated by his list of requirements; if you are young and in
love, you do not want to be reasonable!

So I replied rather tartly:

'If reason is so important, surely all marriages would have
to be marriages of convenience, made for reasons of ex-
pediency rather than love.'

'No,' he replied, still smiling, 'the best marriage is neither
one nor the other, but a *reasonable marriage made for reasons
of love.*'

I was smiling now when I said: 'Yes, I have to admit it!
Once again you have reason on your side.'

The question was too serious, however, for us to leave it
at that.

I went on persistently: 'Even if lovers are quite reasonable

114

and surround themselves with every possible guarantee of success, they are still taking an enormous risk in marrying.'

'Fortunately!' he replied, no longer smiling now. 'If everything could be calculated in advance — something that is fortunately impossible to do — there would be no love. There would be no room for the freedom which is so essential to love.

'It is that freedom which makes it possible for lovers to say to each other: "We have gone a long way together and have taken each other seriously. We have done that in order to get to know each other and to decide whether we can *reasonably* join our two lives together. But I still do not know everything about you and I do not know what we shall become in the future. I do not know how heavy the weight of our suffering will be or how good the experience of our happiness. All the same, I have decided to give you the whole of my life and I think I shall be able to go through with that decision. And I trust you enough to think that you will also give me the whole of your life.

'So there is *a mutual decision* and *a mutual trust* and these provide the real proof of love.'

'But they do not eliminate the risk,' I said again.

'But, as I said before, it is fortunate that there is a risk. If there were no risk, there would be no love. People are afraid to take a risk nowadays and that is very serious. They want an "all risks" insurance policy. They do not want to commit themselves to another person for the whole of their life. I think that points to a lack of maturity and to real weakness.

'If you are afraid to walk, you should never let go of your mother's hand.

If you are afraid of falling, you should stay on your chair.

If you are afraid of an accident, you should leave your car in the garage.

If you are afraid of the climb, you should stay in the mountain hut.

If you are afraid the parachute will not open, you should not jump.

If you are afraid of the storm, you should not weigh anchor.

If you are afraid you cannot build yourself a house, you should leave it as a plan.

115

If you are afraid of losing your way, you should stay
at home.
If you are afraid of making an effort and a sacrifice, you
should stay enclosed within yourself.
If you are afraid of the future, you should give up living.

So you may be able to survive, but you will not be really
human,
because it is human to be able to put your life at risk.
You may be able to pretend to love, but you will not be
really loving,
because loving is being able and wanting to risk your life
for others or for one other.
You may be able to beget a child, but you will not be
really a father or a mother,
because being a father or a mother is being like the grain
of wheat in the earth and risking death so that the corn
may grow.'

I did not want to get involved in argument with my friends,
but I had for some time felt that they were wrong in their
claim that it was better to live with a girl in order to find
out whether their love was quite firm before committing
themselves for the whole of their lives.

Up till now, I had agreed with them and I was not yet so
completely convinced that my changed attitude was right
that I could do without the support of my Friend the Sage.

'Do you think it may be more reasonable to try living
together before committing yourself to a lifelong relationship?'
I asked him hesitantly.

'You must certainly prepare yourself to love, but you cannot try out a relationship of love. As soon as the two people
in love decide to try out their love to see whether it can last,
they are showing one another that their love is not true.'

'But so many couples do act in that way now.'

'They are free to do so. I do not want to judge them.
They have their reasons. But I think they are mistaken. I
do not think they are doing anything harmful. Only the one
who sees into our hearts can say that. But I do not think they
are doing themselves harm and I am sorry for them. They are
not really ready to love.'

116

It was just at that moment that the Child came into the room. My first reaction was to be annoyed with him for interrupting our conversation, because the Sage's eyes left my face at once and followed the Child's movements about the room.

The Child pretended to take no notice of us, but I saw him steal a glance from time to time at the Sage, lowering his eyes each time the Sage looked at him.

Then, quite suddenly, he went up to the Sage, and stood in front of him. He took his hand for a moment in his own, then let it fall and said: 'I do not love you any more, Daddy!'

'I still love you,' the Sage said at once, 'and I shall always love you.'

The Child came closer to the Sage, put his arm round him and kissed him and then went out of the room as quickly as he had come in.

It was obvious that the Sage was delighted by the Child's visits. His face lit up now and the encounter had clearly filled him with happiness.

He broke his long silence to ask me to forgive him for devoting himself so exclusively to the Child.

'A little while ago, I had to refuse to let him do something which he very much wanted to do, but which would have been bad for him and he was sulking when he left me. He came back to me just now to see whether I really loved him. So I had to reassure him. He is like all children — they have to be absolutely certain of the love of those who say they love them.

'A baby cries when he wakes up in the night — cries for his
parents,
to make sure they are still there and have not abandoned
him.
A little child lets go of her mother's hand when they are
out together and walks off on her own, to see whether
her mother will come to look for her.
An older child experiments to see how far he can go
without annoying his parents and when he has broken
all the bonds between them by doing something very
silly, he tries to tie them up again, looking for evidence
that the bonds of love persist.

117

A girl tries to discover how much her parents value her by
calculating the worth of the gifts, the time and the
attention they give her.
An adolescent makes his parents suffer when he tries to
break loose from them and become himself, but at
the same time he is trying to make sure of the
permanence and the authenticity of their love.'

'To hear you speak,' I said, 'I have the impression that
children should not be refused anything they want.'

'On the contrary!' the Sage said. 'We often have to say
no to them. It is not at all good for them to have many of
things they want. But it is important for a child to be quite
certain that "no" does not point to a lack of love. The one
who loves should be able to refuse to give as well as being
able to give.'

'But a baby or a little child cannot understand that refusal.'

'A baby can understand the language of love long before
it can speak.'

'And what about older children and especially adolescents?
They are so often in a state of rebellion!'

'They will understand later, as long as their parents are
disinterested and truthful. Every authentic seed of love sown
in the heart will grow sooner or later and bear fruit.'

'But the seedling can be smothered and killed.'

'Of course. We are free! But although parents are responsible for preparing the ground and sowing the seed, they are
not responsible for the harvest.'

What the Sage was saying interested me, but was, I thought,
a long way from the subject we had been discussing. Almost
as if he divined my thoughts, however, he went on to prove
that I was wrong.

'A grown man is like a child in that he needs the certainty
of being loved if he is to become himself and develop fully.
No one can really believe in his own life and love it unless
he discovers its infinite value. And the one whom he loves
and who loves him more than anyone else is the one who will
reveal that to him.

'In their tender love for their child and their genuine
devotion and firmness, parents will say: "Your life is so

118

precious that we would give our lives for you".

'A lover will say to his loved one: "I chose you from among all the others and you have such enormous value for me that I have decided to give you everything for ever — my heart, my spirit, my body and my whole life."

'But young people are free to say to each other: "Let us try our love out," and who can prevent them from trying? When they are going to try their love out in this way, they do not declare: "We love each other." And they know that, instead of offering each other the most wonderful assurance of all: "I am loved", they are sowing the seeds of the most destructive doubt of all: "Will I ever be loved?" and even: "Am I really lovable?"

'So, my son, that is why I say that we are made by the certainty of being loved and destroyed by doubt about whether we are loved or not. You have to decide whether you want to offer the one you love doubt or certainty.'

26

The Sage was right, of course. No one can live and grow if he is not loved. The world cannot be built up without love. That was something that I had discovered when I first met the Sage. I had lost it for a while, but was discovering it again now.

I had also learnt that people today do not want to risk their lives by loving. That was surely their tragic weakness! Some were willing to try out love, but that just resulted in their becoming exhausted and even breaking down and bringing the world down with them, because they lacked the essential energy that would enable them to live.

Those were my thoughts when I received this poem from the Sage:

Love —
    food for the hungry,
    fresh water for the thirsty,
    warmth for the cold,
    life-blood for the living.

Love —
    poor child in a cruel world.
    We do not trust love.
    We try it out,
    we impose conditions
    and love part-time.

Unhappy world!
    Lacking love you are undernourished.
    Like parched soil you are splitting open —

a world of brothers and sisters who are hostile to each
                                                    other,
a world of enemies exploiting and killing one another.

Unhappy people!
    Torn,
    flayed,
    mutinous,
cut off from love!

People spending their days like dark nights,
    seeking,
    checking,
    calculating:
Have I ever been loved?
Am I loved?
Can I be loved?

People begging for a few mouthfuls of love
    to get through tomorrow,
People seeking pleasure,
    looking for distraction,
    trying to forget their pain,
    and never losing their fears.

Love —
    when will you return to the crazy world
    that does not trust you
    and is slowly dying
    because it does not believe in you?

My God, give me the power to love!
The world needs me and is waiting for me.
Even though I still cannot believe in other people's love
    and even though I still cannot believe in your Love,
at least give me the courage to risk my life for others
    and for one other,
    so that others may not suffer like me.

For all my crazy dreams and my enthusiastic response to
what the Sage had told me, I still did not trust others when

they tried to love me and I still doubted whether I could really love them. I was ashamed of myself for not trusting and recognised this now as my sickness.

Had I ever been really loved? Would I ever be loved in the future? Loved so much by a girl that she would be ready to give her life for me and I would be able to give mine for her?

I asked myself those questions explicitly now, in the realisation that I had, without knowing, been troubled by them for some time and that they had perpetuated the sickness in my heart — that cruel sickness compounded of doubt and lack of trust that had been slowly destroying me. What was the cause of it?

My parents had loved me as well as they could, but quite soon I had begun to notice that they had been less concerned with my happiness than with their own. They had, I realised, been wanting me to satisfy their own desires. When I had not fulfilled their expectations, they had criticised me, not always fairly and often capriciously. The result was that I had come to the painful conclusion that their love for me was no more than a duty. I began by feeling great resentment towards them because of this, took my revenge by making them suffer and ended by being resigned and withdrawn.

But another conclusion was even more damaging: no one was loved for himself and so true love did not even exist! So I had to be satisfied with the little bits of love that I could find on my way.

How eagerly I had looked for those little bits! Not only in friendships with others, but even in the words, gestures and attitudes that I encountered in my everyday life. I was always trying to draw attention to myself! I longed to be admired. I wanted everyone I met to value me and love me.

Everything I said and did was directed — quite unconsciously, of course — to that end. My words, my witty remarks, even my lies and periods of silence, my laughter, my complaints, my acts of gentleness, shyness or aggression, my silent appeals, my noisy demands for attention and even many of my physical weaknesses — they were all so many bottles thrown into the sea in the crazy hope that someone would find them and get the message.

But it had soon become clear to me that it was not enough

122

for me to be noticed, appreciated and loved just by others. Again almost unconsciously, I had soon begun to try to attract the attention of girls. I longed for them to look at me, speak to me, kiss me! I was looking for pleasure, of course, not of the ephemeral kind that ended quickly in disappointment, but of the lasting kind. In other words, I was seeking friendship and love.

But even that search ended again and again in disappointment, because it had not occurred to me that, if I wanted to be loved, I had to be capable of loving.

Then the Sage had entered my life. From the very first meeting, I knew with absolute certainty that he valued me and loved me, that he loved me authentically and unconditionally. He gave me as much time as I needed. He gave me his whole attention. He gave himself totally to me and claimed nothing in return.

I had faith in him and his love and that faith made me want to love. Did I want to love in order to please him? Possibly, but at a much deeper level I knew that, in his presence, I could go beyond myself. His trust in me gave me great confidence. I began to trust and believe in myself because he believed in me. Even my shortcomings could not stand in my way now. I knew that he continued to value me, trust me and love me in spite of them.

I was astonished by the wonderful strength that was coming from me, the mysterious energy that was hidden in the depths of my heart, the Life that had always existed within me. It had been given to me from the beginning, but so far it had remained undetected and had not been able to flow from its source.

The Sage had told me again and again that it had come from elsewhere. That Life and the Love that was hidden within it, he had always said, came from God. Until now, I had grasped the truth of his words with my head. Now I was experiencing it with my heart.

At the same time, I was beginning to recognise the true face of God. Even more than what he said, the Sage's attitude was a living reflection of that face.

God was the one who loved unconditionally. Anyone who was open to that Love and let himself be touched by it would at once be healed. He would stand up, leave his bed

123

and run towards others. I was sure of that now! Just as I was sure that, when Jesus told the sick people in the Gospel: 'Your faith has made you whole,' it was faith in that infinite Love that he meant. It was certainly a healing faith, making it possible for man to 'move mountains'.

Men needed that Love so much. If they were sick and dying, it was because they no longer believed in it.

It was also with that Love that I had to love the other people around me, as Jesus of Nazareth was calling on us to do and as his disciple, the Sage, did.

It was with that Love that I had to love the one who would agree to love me. I knew that now and longed for it with all my heart.

But one question remained: Would I be faithful to her? Faithful throughout the whole of my life? How could I believe in that?

27

When I next saw the Sage, I asked him about lifelong fidelity and he said: 'True faithfulness in marriage is not what you think, my son. It is not a restriction imposed by the law, society and the Church or keeping to a contract so as to avoid a severe penalty.

'Faithfulness is an adventure,
    a way to be followed because it has been chosen.
It lives and grows as the love of the couple grows.
It is that love going forward,
    the daily bread of that love and the wine of its happiness.'

The Sage paused for a moment and said: 'Love does not come to us complete. It has to be made,' then resumed:

'Love is not a ready-made garment,
    but a piece of material to be cut and tailored.
It is not a flat ready for occupation,
    but a house to be designed, built, furnished and repaired.
It is not a conquered peak,
    but a daunting ascent with many obstacles and falls
    made in the icy cold or the fierce heat,
It is not safe anchorage in a harbour of happiness,
    but a voyage on the open sea in storm and tempest.

It is not a triumphant "yes", an affirmation of success,
    a magnificent final chord followed by clapping and cheers,
    but "yes" repeated again and again throughout life
    accompanied by "no" repeated as many times, but
                                   overcome.

It is not the sudden appearance of a new life,
   perfect from the moment of its birth,
   but the flowing of a river from its source,
   sometimes in flood and sometimes only as a trickle of
                                   water,

   but always on its way to the infinite sea.'

The Sage paused a second time to say: 'Faithfulness does not come to us complete. Like love, it has to be made. Faithfulness cannot be separated from love. They go on their way together.

'Being faithful is not
   never losing one's way,
   never fighting,
   never falling.
It is always getting up and going on again.
It is wanting to follow to the end the route
   that you have decided on and mapped out together.
It is trusting each other,
   beyond the darkness and shadows.
It is supporting one another,
   beyond the falls and bruises.
It is having faith in the total power of God's Love,
   beyond human love itself.

Faithfulness is very often the faithfulness of Jesus,
   who was nailed to the cross,
   his body and heart tortured by man's lack of faith-
                                 fulness,

   alone,
   abandoned,
   betrayed,
but who remained faithful to death,
giving and forgiving,
offering his life for us
and saving Love for ever.'

'Yes,' I said, almost inaudibly. 'That may have been possible for Jesus, but can we love like that, to the end, when we experience lack of faithfulness and when we are abandoned and betrayed? No, it is impossible for us to love faithfully to the point of death!'

'We cannot do it alone,' the Sage said, 'but we can with Jesus Christ.'

'But then we have to believe in him!'

'My dear boy,' the Sage replied, 'Through his Son, God is with all those who have ever decided to love each other faithfully. He is our Father. He loves all his children and he loves all those who love each other.'

'What about those who do not love one another?'

'He goes on loving them.'

'So there can never be a complete breakdown?'

'If we want to avoid it — since the cross, no, never!'

I was silent for a long time, unable to reply, then I simply repeated: 'No, it is impossible for us to love like that!'

'I think you will understand later, my son. It took me a long time to understand.'

'You can understand with your head, possibly. But if your heart is deeply touched, how can the pain ever be overcome? It is easy enough to speak if you have not suffered.'

The Sage was troubled by what I was saying. I should have stopped at once, but instead I persisted obstinately:

'How did you come to understand, then?'

To my surprise, he replied at once:

'Through my own experience!'

I felt suddenly panic-stricken, as if I had made a movement and had opened an old wound in my friend's heart.

He neither spoke nor moved. I looked at him, trying to measure from the expression on his face the depth of the suffering that I had revived in him. All I could tell was that I had made his heart bleed, because he was weeping.

What could I say or do? I was paralysed by the shame I felt. When I had recovered sufficiently, I stood up, approached him nervously and put my hand over his. The physical contact reassured me.

'I am sorry. I just did not know.'

'How could you know?' he replied and his eyes told me that he was not resentful.

'My tears,' he said eventually, 'are tears of peace, not of despair or rebellion. They are fruitful tears! Not like those I shed in the past. They ate into my heart like acid. When your heart is wounded, your tears remain, but you cannot grow if they are not transformed into a source of new life.'

He stood up — a clear sign that he wanted me to go.

'It was in that way that Jesus gave us Life, going beyond our lack of faithfulness. I will tell you what I mean by that — but later, not now. I cannot tell you now.'

28

I felt very bad about myself. Despite the Sage's comforting words and reassuring glances, I had the painful impression that I had placed the heavy cross that he had just put down back on his shoulders.

I have to admit it — I felt very dismayed and, even worse, totally disappointed in him. So he too had experienced the defeat and failure of a broken marriage. That was something I had never imagined.

I felt bad about his wife too and at first blamed her. Then I was ashamed of myself for having condemned her so quickly, without even knowing her or the circumstances and found myself blaming him. Anticipating a hard struggle ahead, this feeling of shame was at once followed by one of deep discouragement.

Yes, he was the one who was responsible for the breakdown in the relationship! It was not his wife but he who should be judged. If the Sage had failed in love and marriage, who could possibly succeed? I thought of all the couples I had known whose marriages had collapsed like a house of cards. I thought of the frightening statistics of the increasing number of divorces. And once again I was filled with doubts. This time I felt I would never lose them.

But I recovered surprisingly quickly and became quite proud of myself, counting my reaction as a kind of victory — a proof that I had become stronger and firmer.

I could hear the Sage speaking to me now, even though he was not with me at all. I heard him quite clearly: 'Have I not told you again and again how difficult it is? Do not waste any more time weighing your chances of success in love and thinking at one moment that you may fail and at another feeling proud of yourself because you will be more successful than others! Act now and prepare yourself for it!

'You cannot pass an examination if you have not studied for it. It is hardly possible to practise a profession if you have not learnt it! No one would enter for a race without having trained for it. So how can people imagine that it is possible to found a stable and happy family if they have not prepared themselves for it? It is just not enough to say "I love you" if you want to love someone for the whole of your life.'

'Hearing' these words encouraged me enormously to try again.

Yet I dreaded the next encounter with the Sage! And at the same time I longed to see him again! Another meeting would, I felt, put me at my ease, although I knew I would have to approach it carefully if I was to benefit from it. What I regretted most of all was my judgment of my Friend.

So my first words on seeing him were: 'I am sorry!'

He seemed surprised.

'But how could you know?' he said, repeating the words he had said towards the end of our previous meeting.

'I am not referring to that,' I said, hesitating.

'Have no fear,' he urged me. 'You know you can tell me everything.'

'I am sorry because I ceased to trust you for a while. You appeared to be different from the person I thought you were.'

'You should never cease to trust another person, whatever he may appear to be. But you should also never think the other person is perfect. If you make a god of him, you will sooner or later find out he is only a human being. Loving someone is loving him as he is, with all his strengths and his weaknesses.'

I felt enormously relieved. His words and his very presence had set me free and I wanted to tell him: 'I love you!' but I dared not. I only hoped with all my heart that my smile would reveal that love to him.

I did not ask him to, but he broke the silence, knowing what I wanted to hear from him and speaking slowly and with obvious pain.

'My wife left me for another man. She thought she loved him more than me. She went off taking part of me with her. My happiness with her only lasted for a few years, but my suffering has continued. After all, you go on suffering if one of your limbs has been amputated, even if you manage to accept the hard and permanent reality of the loss.

'My heart became a wild landscape full of weeds. I was full of bitterness and bad feelings. I knew what it was to hate. I had to struggle with all my strength to find peace again. It only returned to me when I learned how to forgive from the depths of my wounded heart. Then love returned as well — a delicate flower that I could only keep alive with a great deal of effort and care.

'Now I still love her and she is still my wife. I pray for her, that she may be happy. And I pray for his happiness too, despite everything.

'Had I done everything I could to make her happy when she was with me? I thought I had, but who can ever say, when his marriage has broken down, that he has not failed in one way or another?

'I went over the path that we had followed together a hundred times in an attempt to discover where I had gone wrong. It was not difficult to find several serious mistakes.

'No one had shown me the way. No one had pointed out the obstacles. And no one had shown me how to prepare myself for the partnership and how to overcome the difficulties.

'And she herself believed that a home could be built up simply on kisses!

'Can you understand now,' the Sage said, looking directly at me, 'why I have told you so many times that loving is difficult and that it takes a long time to learn how to love? If only others did not have to repeat my mistakes and suffer the pain that I have suffered!'

'And how you must have suffered,' I said.

'Yes, I have suffered from my own pain and later from that of other people.'

'What do you mean?' I asked him.

'When I was finally at peace again, I discovered that my time of testing could be very fruitful. My heart had been broken, but it had been healed again. When it had been set free from bitterness, anger and hatred and had begun to beat normally again, I found that it contained a love that was more pure and true.

'So I decided that I would from then onwards be wedded

131

to solitude. In that way I would keep my heart for those who came to me seeking relief from their suffering and would offer them freely the bread they had so far been deprived of.

'And they came to me! I did not have to seek them out. More and more people knocked at my door. I opened my door to them and let them in and suffered with them. I discovered that, when you really love others, you suffer with them the pain that they suffer.'

'But they continue to suffer,' I said.

'Yes, they do, but their suffering is less when it is borne by two people. That is something that Jesus has taught us very clearly by his own example. He offered himself to us in order to bear our suffering with us. In his Love, He gives new Life to those who give him their mistakes and their sufferings.'

Then, very quietly, he added:

'I think that I have also given a little life to those who thought their life had been destroyed for ever. My fingers lack skill, but I may have been able to knead a little new bread with some nourishment.'

As I left the Sage, I thought: I have often come to him for that bread and it has certainly nourished me. That is why I am no longer so hungry!

29

The Sage's experience was something that was shared by others, who often reacted badly to it. There were not many people who reacted as he had done — by not resenting solitude after a broken marriage as inhuman, by overcoming bitterness and by accepting suffering. But, as he said, many came to see him and talk about their failure in love with him. I asked him how he helped them to bear their burden.

'What do you say to those who confide in you?' I asked him.

'I say nothing. I just listen to them.'

'And what do you do when they have finished speaking?'

'I go on listening.'

'Do they go on talking?'

'Oh yes. Often at great length,'

'But what do you say when they have come to the end of their story?'

'I say to them what you said to me: "How you must have suffered." I say no more than that. I just offer them to God in prayer.'

'And what do they say to you?'

'Many different things. Each one has a different story.

He says:

    If my heart is still beating, it is not beating for her.

    For a long time my body has not hungered for her body.

She says:

    He is not the man I dreamed of, the man I married.

    He has hidden his face from me and when I kiss him,

                        I am kissing a mask.

He says:

When I married her, she welcomed me with a warm heart
and tender words.
She never kept anything from me.
But now she is cool and silent and I can no longer
endure her reproaches.

She says:

The flowers in my garden are wilting and he no longer
waters them.
He prefers to visit other gardens and pick other flowers.
And I have trampled angrily on my fallen petals.

He says:

She filled my head with the noise of her words and
could no longer hear the whipser of mine.
And my words, the glowing lava from the volcano of my
heart, erupt violently, burning to ashes what is left
of our love.

She says:

Our children cannot bear our violence any more.
We have put up a tent for them in the storm, but they
are very afraid and the lightning has torn into the
depths of their hearts.

He says:

She held me so firmly in her arms and would not let
me go.
I could hardly breathe or struggle to escape.
When I did find freedom from her, I had to run far away
in search of a space where I could breathe again.

She says:

He kept what he should have said imprisoned in his head.
He built a high wall with the hard stones that his
words had become — so high that we could not
climb over.

He says:

Habit had made its home in both of us.

134

We had for a long time lived in a mist that had hidden
            our smiles and destroyed the taste of our kisses.
We had become old and had ceased to see each other.
We did not recognise each other any more.

She says:

He wanted me for himself and I wanted him for myself
            and we fought constantly to keep one another.
But when the struggle was over, to our surprise
            all that was left of the other in our hands
                        was a few shreds of clothing.

They say:

Why do we go on fighting?
We had heaven yesterday, but today we have hell.
Heaven is love and hell is the absence of love.
We do not want that hell. It is a dead-end.

'It is words like these that I gather in silence in the chalice
of my heart,' the Sage went on.

'Poor sad words, the sounds made by wounded lives,
bleeding as they cross the banks of their bruised lips.

'Often, at the end of the day, when I offer it to the Lord,
my cup is overflowing . . .'

'But when you come to speak,' I persisted. 'What do you
say to them?'

'They have become my very dear friends and I say this
to them:

One of you has gone away, while the other weeps and
            curses and whispers: "I still love you."
Or else both of you wear smiling carnival masks to cover
            your wounded features
and, with the consent of the law, agree to put out the
            last glowing embers of love in the hearth you
                        once shared
and to close the door of your home for ever.

But whether you weep or smile or curse and insult each
                                                      other
   and whatever you do to build happiness elsewhere
   and to light another fire in another hearth,
my dear friends, my poor friends, I have to tell you this:

            You can never get unmarried.

You can tear up your photographs and destroy your gifts.
You can trample on your happy memories
   buried under the weight of unhappy times.
You can even try to share with another what was once
                                    between the two of you.

But you cannot give back the life your partner once
                                              gave you.
   It runs through your veins and is mixed for ever with
                                              your blood,
      going deeper than those caresses you once received,
      and penetrating into the flesh of your heart and
                                              blood vessels.

            You can never get unmarried.

You have tied the threads of your life into the life
                                        of your child
   and that sacred knot can never be untied.
It is the knot of your two lives, united for ever in a new life.
And when you kiss the face of your child,
   you are kissing your own faces as well as that child's.

            You can never get unmarried.

You can blame each other, society or fate.
You can curse the Church and even almighty God.
But his power can do nothing against your freedom.
In freedom, you asked God to commit himself with you
   when you committed yourself to each other,
   and he will remain faithful.

            And he can never unmarry you.

                        136

'That is very hard!' I exclaimed.

'Have I ever said that it was easy to be a free, responsible human being?'

'But men and women are weak. We make mistakes.'

'We are weak, yes, and no one is right to criticise us for our weakness, because no one can ever measure the love that lives in our hearts or know how responsible we are for spoiling that love. But, at the same time, no one can tell us to take back the life that we have given to another person. That life has become the other person's!

'I cannot say it emphatically enough: those who have in freedom given their lives to each other are married in eternity.'*

But I was still not satisfied and pressed him further:

'If you talk in that way to those who come to you with their marriage in pieces, I doubt whether they leave you feeling hopeful and encouraged!'

'If I gave way to weakness and did not talk to them in that way, I would not be respecting or loving them. But, of course, I have other things to say to them as well.'

'Do they come back to hear those other things?'

'Yes, they come back. Like patients coming back to a doctor who speaks the truth to them.'

But I did not want to hear those other things today. I was too deeply troubled.

I was very glad to be a free human being, but I knew that, like all others, I had faults. How could I ignore the enormous mess that we had made of our world? We were so quick to defend our wonderful freedom, but we were quite incapable of managing it!

Like all my fellow-creatures, I wanted God to leave me completely free to choose my own way of life. But, at the same time, I also wanted that God to be a kind parent

---

*On earth, the body is the first means of union between man and wife: they communicate by means of words, tender gestures and embraces. But when two bodies are lawfully united, they cannot be disunited for the sake of another union. In other words, a body cannot be shared. It has richness, but it is also a limitation, which ends only with the death of one of the partners. That is why the Church can remarry widows or widowers if they ask for it.

But, after death, our resurrected life will be quite different. Our bodies will be 'transformed' or 'spiritualised' and will take their place within the relationship between man and wife – a place that will itself be quite different and released from the limitations of matter. (See Mt 19.2-9; Lk 20.27-36; 1 Cor 7.39-40; 15.35,49)

who would cancel out my mistakes and give his blessing to my new choices.

But that was not possible.

We have only one choice when we decide to marry and found a family — either we have to give up being free or we have to accept the risks that freedom involves.

This time I really understood, but even now I would not admit it.

I wanted to be human and free — but I was still afraid.

I did not dare to tell the Sage yet. I had to think about it first.

30

So many couples separated from each other! So many marriages broken beyond repair! Even among the people I knew personally, there were so many failures that I wondered whether successful marriages were not the exception rather than the rule.

I could certainly understand why the Sage insisted so much on the need for young people to prepare themselves for marriage. Who could begin to love without knowing what it was to love and without learning how to love?

I was full of admiration for those who were called to commit themselves in freedom for the whole of their lives and I marvelled at God's infinite respect for their decision. He agreed to put the seal of his Love on their love if they asked for it.

But there were so many failures! And so many painful consequences!

The Sage had assured me that, if we wanted to avoid it, there could never be, since the cross of Christ, a complete breakdown. I wanted that to be true with all my heart, but I could not see how it could be so, since my Friend had also said very emphatically that men and women could not get unmarried in order to try out a second marriage.

So, once again, I had to ask him to explain himself.

He told me:

'Love is like a grain of wheat,
  buried and forgotten in the darkness of the earth.
To the living it seems as though it has died.
But it is not a true death that proclaims life
  if the seed is not watered by the rain and warmed by the
                                                        sun.

The seasons of love are the seasons of life.
Some find the winter mild if they protect themselves
from it.
Others find it cruel as their illusions are dispelled
and the icy wind of disillusion blows through their life.

Spring is a happy time,
a feast of flowers and the promise of fruit to follow.
But sometimes spring can be disquieting,
bringing intoxicating flavours to distracted hearts.

Summer is harvest-time for those who have worked long
hours
and have laboured in the trust they have sown.
And sometimes it lights the flame of noonday loves
making souls dry and setting bodies with hot life-blood
on fire.

Gardeners of love, you must know that love can
be grown
and many whom you may think dead or dying
are alive.'

'But so many people are ignorant and do not know how to
grow such plants,' I said. 'So their sick love can hardly survive.'
'There are doctors of the heart,' the Sage replied, 'Those
who live close to God, reliable friends, who can care for
those sick loves.'
I understood what the Sage meant by this. I thought of my
own parents and the number of times they might have avoided
conflict and suffering if they had let someone help them to
understand each other and themselves and if they had been
allowed to marry just as they were and not as they wanted
each other to be.
But it was clearly too late for so many married couples!
They had already buried the love that they believed was
dead and were trying to make another love grow on the
earth that had been trodden hard. But how could they
succeed if God rejected them?
When I told the Sage what I was thinking, he rose angrily
to his feet.

140

'That is quite wrong!' he exclaimed. 'God never rejects us. We move away from him!'

'What should they do, then, those lovers whose marriage is broken and who have chosen another partner?'

'They should first acknowledge their weakness and then pray to be given Light.'

'But how?'

'Like suffering children:

Understand me, God, you who understand so well
    both your faithful and your sinful children.
I have not been able to live alone, lost and abandoned —
    my heart was too cold
    and my body too hungry.

How could I sail alone on a stormy sea
    with a broken mast and sails torn,
without looking for someone to help me repair my ship
    and continue the voyage with me.

How could I, as a woman, feed my disabled children alone,
    while they were crying for my mother's milk
    and I was wounded, the blood of love flowing from me
    and my breasts quite dry.

I could not, God, refuse the little love that I was offered
    and the few shreds of happiness put in my empty hands.
I tried to make another nest to replace the one destroyed
    and I dare not leave my new love
    in case he flies away from me like a frightened bird.

Despite my wounds and the burden I bear,
    I am, I think, happy at last,
    like a rainbow in the sky full of clouds.
Do not destroy my happiness, God, I beg you!

But I am afraid and full of doubts,
    because I hear that you cannot bless this new home.

Why, my God, oh why is it wrong
    to try to be happy after having suffered so much?

Love me, God! Do not abandon me!
 I need your love so much.
I am trying to love more perfectly now
 and want to offer you these crumbs of new love
 which are, I believe, really love.

'And what is God's reply to this?', I asked

'I waited for a long time to learn it,' the Sage said. 'We are often discouraged by what we think is the silence of God. But it is wrong to think he does not speak. I know that he does, but that we often do not listen to him.

'I have listened. I have tried to make my heart so pure that I could hear him whispering. Then I was able to convey the reply that I believed I could hear to those who came to the door of my house — the door of my heart.

'I believe that this is God's reply:

My child, I have always loved you and I still love you.
A true father never rejects his child,
 even if he is a prodigal son
 and moves away from him.

You could not live alone and I understand your weakness.
You have decided and it was your decision.
You are free — in my love for you, I want your freedom.
But I cannot untie the bond that we have tied between us.
Even my Church can do nothing to break my bond of
                                        marriage —
 it can only sometimes say there was no marriage.
  I am Love
  and Love is faithful
 and you can never make me say I am unfaithful!

My dear child, you are suffering and I understand your
                                        pain.
 I accept your prayer and even the violence of your words,
 for who can pray calmly when his heart is bleeding
  and his body is torn?

But do you not know, my child, that your suffering is mine?
My cross was not yesterday — it is also today
    and it will be tomorrow.
My Passion is more than blows, thorns and nails —
    it is the infinite suffering of Love that is mocked.

They have not finished nailing me to the cross
    and my arms are stretched out to the end of time.

But my arms end in my hands, and they are wide open,
    and I am carrying each of you separately
    and my heart is at the centre uniting you for ever —
    a living heart that continues to love.

Trust in me, my child, and do not be afraid to come to me —
    there are many ways to me and from me to you.
Accept the pain of separation!
Like my divided Church, you cannot bear witness to unity,
    but the pain of disunity may bear witness to the greatness
                                                    of unity!

But, my very dear child, recognise your mistakes and your
                                                    weakness.
    Ask for forgiveness
    and forgive those whom you must forgive
    for love cannot live in a heart that is closed.

And give me your hesitations about your new love
    and I will accept them on my cross
    and take care of everything.'

I think that I grasped the essential message that the Sage
was giving me today. It was that God suffers in Christ crucified because of our disunity and divisions, but, if we want
him to, he will save us by loving us for ever.

31

I was, as usual, sitting face to face with my friend. I knew that he needed to look at me and I wanted his eyes on me.

I was going to speak, but before I could, the Child came into the room. He kissed the Sage and then walked round the room touching various objects and opening drawers containing pencils, rubbers and dozens of other little treasures that had been left in them because there was no other place to put them. He clearly felt very much at home as he was looking for what he could use himself in the drawers. His presence obviously amused the Sage and made him very happy.

I had a few sweets in my pocket and offered him one. He seemed surprised, but took the sweet, thanked me and went out of the room sucking it.

Meanwhile, the Sage continued to look at me. His eyes were pensive and, I thought, a little sad.

'The Child does not really need your sweet so much as your attention and, yes, your affection.'

'But he obviously wanted the sweet,' I said. 'I could see that as soon as I offered it to him.'

'He wanted it, but was it really necessary for him? His desire will be satisfied and be revived as soon as he has eaten the sweet. He will be back in a moment for another sweet and expect you to give it to him. Adults so often give children what is not essential, but deprive them of what is essential.'

'Surely that is because they love them and want to give them pleasure.'

'Unfortunately it is often because they want to be loved themselves and even because they want to be forgiven.

'It is not sweets, but love that enables children to live and grow. So many children do not grow or else grow up badly because they are not loved or else loved badly . . .

The child who is buried beneath toys and unable to
        breathe and has no more to long for because all his
            wishes have been satisfied even before they appeared
                and developed.
The only child whose parents refuse to have the longed-
        for brother or sister, because they want a new house,
            a new car or an additional holiday.

The child condemned to sit at table in the restaurant,
        restless because of an over-filled plate, while the
            parents never stop eating, drinking and talking —
                so long as they also do not stop being bored.
The child sitting in the back of the car, weary and longing
        for freedom, imprisoned in the moving home of the
            families of adults who can no longer walk.

The child left alone during the day because the parents
        want to work for him, and left alone in the evening
            because they are generously caring for the whole world
                and other people's children.
The child saturated with sounds and images, left sitting
        in front of the television screen, spellbound, like a moth
            flying again and again into a square of light.

The child, the intelligent animal, running every day from
        school to a music lesson or games practice, with no
            time to play, to be idle or to dream.
The child whose play is already orientated towards work
        and whose participation in important causes is already
                sought by adults
and who always plays alone, inventing partners for
                dream games.

The child who is not allowed to get dirty, to speak or
        even to move, and the child who is allowed to do every-
            thing because of being the parents' only treasure and
                because they think that this is how to keep him.

145

The child with parents like eider-down, beaten with fists
                                                  and words,
and the child with concrete parents who make no response,
            however much small fists bleed, hitting them.

The child who does not know why she is there and why
      she is alive, because her parents do not know themselves,
   or because they had her by accident and, after hesitating,
                        decided to let her live after all,
or because they "felt like" having a child one day,
or because you get married in order to have a child,
or because everyone else has a family,
or because babies are so lovely,
or because a baby can bring you together if you have
                                          moved apart,
or because a family is a guarantee that you will not be
                  alone when you are old — or die alone.'

The Sage was clearly carried away by what he was saying. He had stood up and was speaking very forcibly. It was
as if he wanted to be heard by adversaries a long way away.
His eyes were blazing with anger.
   'You are very severe!' I said.
   'Forgive me.' He calmed down at once. 'It hurts me to see
children spoilt. Children are so beautiful!

'*Child*,
      two bloods mingled
      two lives mingled
      two hearts mingled.
      Man and woman joined for ever, united
            in their love made flesh.

Child,
      unique work of art,
      inestimable treasure,
      new star shining in the sky
            among countless millions of equally necessary stars,
      "you" — a person appearing only once and for the first
                                                        time
      and unrepeatable.

Child,
  loved by man,
  blessed by God,
  externally desired by the Father,
  assuming a body
  when, marvellously, human love and freedom meet desire.

Child,
  the child of man and woman,
  the child of God,
  a member of an unfinished Body
  but cut off from it without You,
    Body of humankind,
    Body of Christ,
  growing since the beginning of time on earth
  and rising up to heaven.

How was it possible for God,
  in the incomprehensible foolishness of his love,
  to give men and women the power —
    in their bodies the life-force
    in their hearts the desire —
  with him to create you,
  to create you, the new life,
  you, the new source pouring out over this earth —
    this world of human life —
  the beginning of a great river flowing into eternity?

Parents, do you know?
When you were made rich by the life you had received,
  a life that had become yours because it was given to you,
you did not want to live like parasites
  on that treasure that was a gratuitous gift
  without handing it on gratuitously.

When you had increased in love, body and soul,
  you gave yourselves to one another,
  welcoming the unique gift that the other could give you.
And when you were saturated with the life that was offered,
  you refused to keep it to yourselves, jealously guarded.

When the life-force in your veins, warm and palpitating,
    began to desire the flower and look for the fruit,
your bodies, trembling with pleasure in the bed of life,
    and your hearts, beating in joyous anticipation,
    opened the way for that life-force — the way to the child.

Parents, do you know?

Fulfilling the loving expectation of your Father in heaven,
    you have been surrounded by his infinite joy.

But you should never forget —
    once you have really given that life,
    you can never ask the child to give it back to you.
Your life has become another life.
    It is that child,
    for ever.

When your task of bringing them up is completed,
    they will leave the bosom of the family,
    just as they once left their mother's bosom.
        Your hearts will bleed,
        just as Christ's body was bled,
        but there will be joy —
        the joy that they will in their turn
        give the life that has been given to them.

'So, my son,' the Sage said, 'it is a great joy for parents
who have been really loving to have children, because love
comes from God and God expects it to bear fruit. But the
seed has to break open and the petals of the flower have to
fall before that fruit can appear. So giving life is also accepting suffering while accepting joy.'

32

I was happy now because I had begun to understand both the greatness and the beauty of the child and the responsibility of the parents.

I remembered how, as a young man, I had been troubled about my own origins and whether my parents had been really glad to have me or whether they had regarded my coming into the world as a nuisance. But that did not seem to matter now. I was happy because I had discovered the essential truth — that God had wanted me with an infinite longing.

I began to dream of meeting a girl and of making a child with her, a child we longed for as God longed for him. . . .

Had the Sage experienced the happiness of being a parent? I asked myself this question, but hesitated to put it to him. But as soon as I was confronted with him again, it came quite naturally to my lips.

'Have you ever had a child?' I asked him point-blank.

'I have never had a child of my own flesh, but I have had many children of my heart!'

'And the Child I have seen here? You seem to love him so much. Is he one of those children of your heart?'

'Yes, he is. He is also deeply wounded. He sees his mother sometimes and occasionally he meets his father, but he never sees them together. His heart has been damaged by his parents' separation. Love has been injured and the wound is still bleeding. I have tried to heal it, but it is still there, even though it is hidden.'

'You have tried to console him?'

'No, I tell him the truth: "You have suffered and you will continue to suffer, but you are able to make your life succeed and to save your parents' love."

'Wounded child of separated parents,
  you are the crossroads where the roads divide,
    the meeting-place for hearts at night-time.
  You are the knot that cannot be untied,
    the flesh that cannot be divided.
  You are your father and mother
    who cannot be divorced in you
    and whose love survives as long as you live.
  You are those two, married for ever.

Abandoned child of unknown parents,
  you are the face of your mother and father,
    who for you are without faces or names.
  You are new life, born of human longing,
    fulfilling the longing of God.
  You are more than the child of your parents —
    you are his child, the child of the Father,
    because you are open to his Love.

Wounded and abandoned children,
  if you are willing,
  the Father will bring you up
  as his beloved children,
  because a place has been made in you
  that is waiting for him
  and is not disputed by your parents,
  who often think they know better
  than the Father of life.

Wounded and abandoned children,
  you must live!
Live with all your body and all your heart
  and, if you can,
  pray to your Father:

Here I am, my God,
  my Father, faithful in love,
  in your presence!
I fully possess my life
and I am in control of my future.

150

This life is mine
because it was given to me —
   or abandoned to me.
I accept it
   and I accept my suffering.
I accept the suffering of my broken branches,
   even though I do not know the roots of my tree.
The sun of your Love, Lord, shines on us all,
   piercing the thickest clouds,
   ripening the fruit borne by my tree,
   and all I have to do is to live in the daylight
   and avoid the bitterness and sombre regrets of night.

Help me to live, my God, and to make my life succeed,
   so that the children I may have tomorrow may live.
I may not have been fully loved by a united mother and
                                             father,
   but, by measuring the depths of the injury done to me,
   I have learned how much they needed to love.
And I know now how painful suffering can be,
   but also how much we can learn from it.

Help me to live, my God, and to make my life succeed,
   so that my parents may live in and through me.
I am, after all, their love made flesh,
   even if that love was no more than momentary.

Help me to grow, my God,
   so that they may grow.
Help me to love, my God,
   so that they may love.
Help me to give my life, my God,
   so that their life may be fruitful.
And mysteriously and in silence,
   with you, my Father,
I will beget my mother and father,
I will give them life,
I will bring them up
and I will save them
   by saving their love.'

When the Child came into the room again for another sweet, as the Sage had said he would, I did not give him one this time. I hugged him and, taking his hand, spoke and listened to him.

33

I could not help being amazed by the change that had recently
taken place in me. At one time, I used to try to calculate the
quantity and quality of the pleasure a girl might give me. This
was followed by a search for the tenderness she could offer.
I had by then discovered that I was not simply full of desires
that demanded to be satisfied. I also had a sensitive heart
and was lonely. I wanted to be loved.

But I was still in the centre of the world! I was still looking
for my own happiness! I still had not learned that I would
only find it if I went out of myself and tried to make other
people — and one other person — happy.

So I had gradually come not to regard girls as objects for
pleasure or even as objects that could provide tenderness, but
to see them as persons who deserved to be fulfilled by me
because of their smile, their heart and themselves. And I
remembered what the Sage had told me — that, if we are to
love, we have to go beyond our desire to take and want to
give and receive. That, then, was the path I had to follow to
the end.

I now knew I would never cease to learn how to love. My
life had changed and it would go on changing if I continued
to learn how to love. This made me very happy and the Sage
saw that happiness.

So he greeted not me, but life itself when I came to see
him.

'Yes,' I said, 'I am alive and I am happy to be alive! And
tomorrow, with my love, I shall — we shall — give life to
children. We shall show them to you and you will see that
we have succeeded.'

But what had I said to make the Sage suddenly so serious?

I was expecting a happy response from him, but he remained silent.

I knew him well enough now to know when his silence indicated happiness and when it reflected sadness. This was a sad silence.

Eventually he said: 'What if you cannot have children?'

'Oh, we shall have children!' I said. 'Doctors can work miracles nowadays. Soon there will be nothing they cannot do.'

'Do not speak like that, my son,' he said. 'A child is not a right, but a gift — the gift of love, when it encounters the infinite Love of the Father of the whole of life.

'It is true that great progress has been made and that men are able to do marvellous things. I am very proud of their achievements, but sometimes disturbed by them.'

'But surely God is not afraid of the power he has given them?'

'He is not afraid of their power, but he may be afraid of the way in which they use it,' the Sage replied gently.

'Men of our generation have discovered the secret of matter and have learned how to harness the great energy it contains. But the first time they made use of that energy they employed it to kill two hundred thousand people. We cannot forget Hiroshima!'

'But scientists put themselves at the service of life when it is a question of childbirth.'

'So long as they never forget that they are not absolute lords of human life. Life will prove to be sterile if they mix it with the yeast of human pride or manufacture it at the bidding of people like yourself who think that they have a right to a child.

'I hear it quivering —
   life in the heaviness of time,
   unfathomable mystery,
   sacred source,
   springing from the burning heart,
   originating in Love.
I hear it flowing —
   life-blood in the veins of mankind.

154

I hear it calling —
    calling for two loving hearts
    in two consenting bodies,
    calling for the bud, the flower and the fruit
    to grow in the sunlight of God.

Do you believe,
    you scientists who do not understand
    the mystery of life,
    that life can be made to appear by chance
    from a clever conjurer's box?
Do you not know
    that the seed that you manipulate
    in your sterilised forceps
    has been made by the joy and suffering
    of countless men,
    and the child who is born
    of your successful experiment
    will never be your creation?
That child is the precious cloth
    woven throughout the centuries
    by skilful weavers of love!
Do you not know too,
    you proud scientists,
    whose fingers are so nimble
    and whose professional skill is so great,
    that you will never be able to create a child
    unless the Creator works with you
    in that creation.

So, if you believe this,
    men of science collaborating with God,
    you should serve life on your knees in prayer and humility
        and perhaps also serve life by celebrating Christ's birth.

        But what do you require of God?
        And will we ever be capable of loving so much
        that we shall be able to give children,
            even before they are born,
        all the love that they need
        and to which they have a right?

Listen to tomorrow's child singing,
   you scientists, and all who are responsible for others:

I am the longing of the loving Father
   and I have been waiting since the beginning of time
      to set off on my long pilgrimage.
I come from elsewhere, a very long way away,
   and I am on the way that I have always been following.

I need all of you,
   my brothers and sisters who have gone before me,
   and who have hollowed out the river-bed of life,
      the bed of my life and your lives.
But I also need two living bodies with hearts,
   singing the love song of two lovers,
   two tender glances,
   hands seeking each other
   and lips meeting, breath mingling.
I need these when, after centuries,
   the banks of many rivers have been crossed,
   before I can stand on the earth,
   before I can utter my first cry,
   before I can smile for the first time,
   before my first words can be expressed
   and my unique message can be heard.
I need "yes" expressed freely
   by those two living bodies and hearts.

If I am to be born at all,
I need a father who will be my father
   and a mother who will be my mother.
I need two loving parents
   who will bear me in their hearts
   long before they bear me in their arms.
I do not want to be born
   of seed selected in a magician's laboratory
   or even of seed given by generous donors,
   unknown people offering what is left over.

I need to be made in a long cry of love,
    an astonishing encounter,
    the root of happiness growing in flesh.
I do not want to be born
    in a heartless test-tube.
I do not want to be the result of a cold embrace
    of parents without arms, lips or living flesh.

I need to be curled up in the warm womb of my mother,
I need the darkness, the shade of her body
    and the closeness of her beating heart
    to give my voyage from the haven its rhythm.
I need my father's hands and lips on my mother's body.
I need his loving words, falling like rain on the shore
    appearing like dew on the buds that are opening.

I do not want a hired womb,
    where I would hear songs I would not continue to hear.
Nor do I want a deep-freeze,
    where I would be alone, waiting for warmth
    — the warmth of whatever love was available —
    seen by eyes that cannot see
    watched by official observers
    who do not know what to do with my countless brothers
                                            and sisters.

When I have finally crossed thousands of obstacles
    and have finally reached the end of my long voyage,
and, when at last I have the courage to risk stepping out
    onto this hard earth and appearing before you
    as a work of art that has been begun, but is not yet
                                                finished,
I shall need the sweat of others on the way to wash me
    and my mother's tears of joy to fall on me.
I shall need to be bathed for the first time in light
    on the beach of her body
and I shall need to explore that body,
    since all that I shall have known of it until now
    will have been the wrong side of night.

157

But I would not like my birth to have been a failure,
  the voyage to have ended in a shipwreck,
  with me thrown up on an unknown island,
  lost among the sound of the waves.

Scientists, do not laugh at those other scientists,
  who will later flick through the pages of our early
                                    memories,
They will be astonished to find in those inexhaustible mines
  memories that you will never see under your blind
                                    microscopes.
Long before we appear on this earth,
  we children can see, hear and feel
and you forget that we forget nothing!

That is yesterday, but tomorrow those memories will be
  the mysterious foundations on which we shall build
                              our lives
    and others will ask why the house is not always firmly
                              built
    and why it sometimes falls down in the storms of life.
You may be skilful enough as potters
  to shape our flesh with the submissive clay,
  but you forget in the process
  that we have a heart in the flesh of our children's bodies.
And that heart is something that you can never shape!

How much I admire you scientists
  and how greatly I value your science!
  I shall, after all, be an adult tomorrow!
But I am afraid too that your skill is increasing
  while your heart is overshadowed, not growing.
Today you are working so hard to make sure that a life
                                    is born,
  but tomorrow you will destroy life in the womb
  because you think it is too fertile.
And you will not hear our cries because they are too weak.
The cries of children will also be drowned by those of
                                    adults
  proudly marching to defend their freedom to experiment.

We children are afraid.
We are afraid of the world we are entering.
Listen to me again,
you scientists
who are responsible for other people!
The truth comes from the mouths of children!

I am a child and I have escaped the slaughter of the night,
   because I was held back by a thread of love,
   though where it came from I do not know.
I am a child who has fallen from the nest
   and my parents may have flown away
   or they may have died from beating themselves
   against the bars of their cage.
I am a child who has the right to live because I am alive,
   but I am wearing borrowed clothes
   and sometimes I go naked, without the clothes of love.

Many couples are unhappy because they are longing for
                                              a child.
They have an abundance of love, but it is not used.
They would like to give it to another
   whom they have not sowed and planted
   so that such a one could grow and bear flowers and fruit.

I would like one of those couples to come and ask me
if I would adopt them as parents of my heart!

There are, however, certain couples that I want to avoid.
There are those who are obsessed with desire for a child,
   who long to possess a perfect object of art,
   a rare piece to complete their collection.
There are also those who have ordered their goods,
   have waited for their prefabricated baby to be delivered
   and, as satisfied customers, have paid the bill.

I was not made to save parents with amputated limbs,
   but they were made to save children
   whose hearts are sick and maybe even ruined.

In the course of this mysterious and magnificent movement,
    we shall be won over.

I shall drink as yet untasted milk.
I shall hear hitherto unknown music.
I shall learn to sing new songs.
I shall slowly decipher on your fingers and your lips,
    my parents whom I have adopted,
    the new alphabet of tenderness
and, in the light of your eyes,
    the love that I do not yet know
    will take on a human face.

You will graft your lives onto my wild growth
    and you will enable me to be reborn.
I will then have two sets of parents —
    two of my flesh and two of my heart and my grown
                                                    flesh.

You will not judge the unknown parents who begot me,
    but will thank them
    and help me to respect them.
I have, after all, to learn to love them in darkness
    if I am ever to love myself in the light.

I may, of course, criticise you harshly for having welcomed
                                                    me
    when I am caught up in the turmoil of adolescence.
Do not be too deeply hurt; and try to love me more!
There has to be a wound if the graft is to take
    and, when the would heals, the scar remains.

But now I am simply dreaming,
    because I am a child on the way
    and still far from land.
My song is without music and I am still unable to speak.
What I am whispering into your hearts
    is something that I cannot yet express in words.

Is it that, on the day that you adopted me,
    you put enough love and freedom into my heart
    and enough words on my lips
    for me to say this:

    My mother and my father —
    I have chosen you
    and I have adopted you.

So you may know that your love is a gift
    and it has succeeded.'

34

After listening to this long meditation I lay awake for a long time during the night, upset by the thought that the child who was waiting to be born might be wounded and spoilt. Many adults were very severe in their judgment of young people, but surely they were to blame? They were only condemning themselves in condemning adolescents. What would my attitude be, I wondered, if I had a family?

This brought me back to the recurrent theme: I should get to know a girl and set up a home with her. Like two musicians playing a duet in public together after practising their parts separately.

In public? That was just the question that I asked myself again and again and that I had so often discussed with my friends. Was it really necessary, if one wanted to set up a home together, to sign the registrar's forms and make declarations in his office or in a church? Did one really have to satisfy the law in this way and was one not in fact only conforming to established practices?

It would be impossible to avoid it without a long struggle with my parents and other members of my family. And that hardly seemed worth undertaking, even though the practices surrounding marriage belonged, in my opinion, to the past. Love between two people was entirely their own affair and their commitment to each other only concerned them.

As for the church wedding, I was now convinced of its necessity, even though I still did not fully understand its significance.

When I spoke to the Sage about my difficulties with the public aspect of marriage, the first thing he said was: 'Two lovers are not alone in the world. Would they really want to be alone?

Would you really want, men and women joined together,
to live alone
in the protected enclosure of your new love?
Would you really want to walk hand in hand along
a private road
and not follow the ways taken by your brothers and
sisters?
Would you really want to be free of all constraints,
stop at the green and go on at the red traffic lights,
eat when others are sleeping and sleep when they
are eating?
Would you really want to build the home of your dreams
alone,
teach your children there and reject public education?
Would you really want to bake your own bread, make
your own clothes,
provide your own lighting and heating?
Would you really want to prepare your own medicines,
perform operations, nurse each other during sickness?

You are free,
but, if you really want to be alone,
you must be prepared to go to a desert island
and die alone there with your love.

Surely you would rather walk hand in hand along a way
chosen from among those already followed by others?
Surely you would rather choose a house others have built
and live in peace there, protected by others?
Surely you would rather eat the bread others have baked
while you were sleeping safely in your beds?
Surely you would rather send your children to school
while you go out to work and get paid for it?
Surely you would rather let others care for your health
and look after you when you were sick,
so that you can bring up your family
and live in peace when you are old.
Surely you would rather have laws to protect those rights,
and people qualified to formulate and administer them?

163

And surely you would rather not be constantly in search
of profit,
exploiting others and treating them as less than human?

If this is so, then, you will commit yourself to society,
which is also committed to you.
Your name will then be added to the list of those who love
and you will be fully a member of that society
which is dedicated to the task of building up the world.

One member of the body can only live
if it is joined to the other members.
If two arms are united to carry a heavy weight,
the other parts of the body share the task.

Love is the blood of humanity's body
and no one can grow without it;
so, when a man and a woman are joined together in a
lifelong covenant,
all humankind is filled with a hidden joy.

'It is above all because of that responsibility for each other,' the Sage said, 'that those who have freely decided to set up a home together must commit themselves in public. Their parents, relatives and friends and the whole of society — we are all, in fact, responsible for the success of their life together.'

'I imagine that is why believers commit themselves in church — in the presence of God?'

'Yes,' the Sage replied. 'For that reason and many others too.'

'Would you tell me about the sacrament of marriage that I hope to receive one day with my love?'

'It is such a great mystery that, if we are to speak about it at all, we need words that are fashioned in gold. The only words I have are very meagre! We also need couples to speak about the sacrament who are experiencing it in the light and I am only trying to experience it in darkness.'

'But I would like you to speak about it all the same. I need to know more if I am to prepare myself for marriage.'

'God has loved us silently since the beginning of time,
   but long ago, wanting to declare that love,
   he chose a people for himself.
But that people was fickle and hard-hearted in its love
                                  for him,
   and again and again unfaithful to him who is Love itself,
   yet again and again forgiven by him who is faithful.

God then chose a Virgin, blessed among women,
   and whispered to her the secrets of Love.
And the word she had meditated in her heart
   took root in her body overshadowed by the Spirit.

     Through Mary, Jesus wedded mankind
     in a perfect marriage,
     a perfect "yes",
     exchanged between God and man,
     a new covenant
     sealed in and for eternity.

God has since that time been among us
   as one of us, our brother.
He has been for us the body of God,
   handed over in Jesus,
   his arms wide open on the cross,
   betrayed by our faithlessness,
the Body of God
   living beyond death,
   our companion for ever,
   going with us, his people, on the way,
the Body of God
   offered in communion
   to those who say "yes"
   to his "yes" inviting us.

It is in that "yes" of the new covenant,
   a "yes" that is greater than the earth itself
   and wider than the river of time
that, since the first men and the first women
   whispered their "I love you" in so many languages,

couples have throughout history
joined the long wedding procession.

And in that long procession,
the way followed by countless believers
goes through the Church of Jesus Christ,
so that the words of fire that commit their lives
may be spoken in the presence of the community.

We know, God, that you are present in our love
and that we receive that immense gift from you —
a gift that we make our own and offer to each other.

We come before you, Lord, to celebrate that love
and to declare it to each other.
We say aloud our "yes" and in it we hear your "yes",
for, when we commit ourselves freely to one another,
you commit yourself with us.

We believe that this double commitment is the sacrament
of Love,
Love given and received by us,
so that our covenant may be made in your covenant with
mankind.

We believe, Jesus, that you were sent by the Father
to reveal to mankind
the infinite nature of the Love of the Trinity
and to give to us a Face that we could contemplate
and words and deeds to satisfy our hunger and thirst.

We believe that, because of this sacrament, we are sent
to each other,
to provide an image of your revealed Love
and to give one another a few crumbs of that Love.

We believe that you have made a covenant with your people,
the Church,
and that you are faithful for ever.
We also believe that our "yes" is the tangible evidence
of your "yes".

166

We believe that you have married the whole of humanity,
   giving your body to make one flesh with us.
and in the joyful union of our flesh and our communion
   your Love can be rooted in the flesh of the world.

We believe that you heal our love when we fall
   and, raising it on the cross, save it from death
and place it within the framework of eternity.

'How can I express the infinite in words?' the Sage concluded. 'And your lives are only a pale reflection of this
great mystery of Love that I would like you to go on contemplating all your life.
   'If you invite Jesus to live with you in your home and try
together to make Love incarnate in this world, you will never
be alone, you and your love.

Heat and light are not made by a twig burning,
   but by a fire formed of many branches.
Some burn out and others catch alight
   and ashes and flames are mingled in the hearth.

Our lives are flames and ashes, but the fire never dies
   and the Love that is kindled at the burning heart of
                                             Jesus Christ
      will never be extinguished.'

167

35

The Sage's words were soothing, but they were also, I thought, too good to be true. I felt like an art-lover looking at a painting and at first seeing only random colours and shapes. Only when the artist himself explains his work can the viewer begin to explore its depths. Every colour and every shape comes to life for him and the picture is revealed as a whole. His illusions vanish, he understands the deeper meaning of the word of art and he recognises sadly that this is something that he as an amateur will never be able to produce himself.

In the same way, the Sage had enabled me to discover the true dimensions of love and again and again I had said: 'That is too difficult for me. You are describing peaks that I shall never be able to climb.'

So it was for me today. After leaving the Sage, I had thought about the sacrament of marriage and had come to the conclusion that it pointed to a way of experiencing married life with Jesus Christ that was a form of responsibility going far beyond my power, rather than a companionship that might strengthen me.

I was also deeply discouraged and even irritated and disgusted by another aspect of the relationship between man and woman. Right-minded people were always declaring that certain acts in that relationship were wrong or evil, although they seemed quite normal to me. Then I was very conscious of the voice of the Church with its prohibitions and the media, greedy for sensation and apparently condemning everything.

Love seemed to me to be a minefield that very few people could cross without risking injury or death!

And yet all around me were people smiling and laughing, going blithely on their way and apparently quite indifferent to these condemnations.

168

But my Friend did not condemn or forbid and that was why I went on listening to him. Yet his words disturbed me much more than those prohibitions. I could not laugh about his words and it was I who had to decide whether or not to change my life. I was ashamed to admit it to myself, but the truth was that I would have been happier if I had remained in darkness.

But, despite all this, I continued to question my Friend.

Going to see him later that day, I found a young woman in his home.

'My nurse,' he said and introduced her to me. I hardly looked at her. I felt suddenly anxious. Was he ill — perhaps seriously? He told me at once that he just had a temperature and I was at once reassured. I said I would go, but he asked me to stay.

'There is something else I want to tell you,' he said, adding archly: 'and I also want to reassure you.'

I was no longer astonished now that he seemed always to know how I felt even before I spoke. It pleased me, because his insight into my feelings revealed his love for me.

I listened attentively to what he said.

'Love is a peak reaching up to heaven
     and that heaven is the family of Father, Son and Spirit,
          the family of God that is infinite Love.
We shall only be able to love with the love that exists
                                                    in God
     when we are all perfectly united as brothers and sisters
          in Jesus Christ our brother
     and when he was brought us to share with him
          the wedding banquet of eternal love.

The path to the top of that mountain is winding.
     It has many turnings, goes up and down
          and often leads to rock faces.
The couple who undertake the ascent may go astray
     and no one can fly to the summit like an arrow!
We cannot fly — we are only learning how to walk.
And we can only learn how to love on the roads of our
                                               daily life.

169

How many impetuous couples, dazzled by their own
happiness,
forget that the valley is a long way from the summit!

Eager lovers look tentatively for words and gestures
that will feed their love on its long journey,
but many mistakes accumulate
in their hearts made narrow and their bodies heavy
by lingering selfishness.

Some love stories are full of faults,
but they are no less precious in the eyes of Jesus Christ
so long as those who are writing them are trying to
learn
humbly and faithfully from him how to express their
love.

The guide has to remind the climbers again and again
not only that their starting-point is not the end of
the climb,
but also that their mountain is only one among many.
It would be a poor guide who did not do this,
warning those unpractised climbers, also, of the length
of the ascent,
the difficulties of the rock faces
and the risk of falling,
and speaking only about the purity of the mountain air,
the warmth of the sun's rays,
the flowers they would gather on the way up
and the splendour of the view from the top.

Some couples set off alone without an experienced guide,
avoiding the paths traced by others before them.
They laugh at what they call conventional morality,
taboos and restrictions, and call themselves liberated.
They claim that they are sensible enough
to dispense with a map and compass,
and go climbing without food and drink.
"Our feeling for mountains is our best guide," they say.

170

But are they sensible?
Who can reach the summit
  without knowing the safest way,
  and the dangerous scree slopes and crevasses?
Who can even drive safely to the top
  without observing the road signs
  indicating dangerous bends, "falling rocks",
  maximum speeds and "no entry"?
Who can ignore the advice of those who know the way
  simply because they have already planned their route?

No, they are not sensible!
Can the athlete ever become a champion
  by rejecting the rules of the game
  and the programme outlined by the trainer?
Can the soloist ever give a good performance
  while ignoring the conductor and the other musicians,
  neither in tune nor in time with the orchestra?
Can the tree ever grow to its full height
  if it is not planted in good soil,
  in the light and exposed to the rain
  or if it is not separated and grafted early enough,
  staked and regularly pruned?

'There are rules of the game in love,' the Sage said. 'Love has its own laws and, if they are broken, it becomes sterile and may even die.'

'But surely love is not just a set of rules to be followed or laws to be obeyed! Everything you have said shows me it is more than that!'

'Of course, you are right. Loving is not simply following rules. It is following Someone. It is following Jesus Christ, the one John called quite simply Love.

'Rules and moral laws are only norms and indications making our encounter and our life together with Jesus Christ possible. We have to respect them if we do not want to go astray. But we must never forget that he is the true Guide. He called himself the 'shepherd'. And he looks in the valley for volunteers to accompany him on his ascent to the top of the mountain.

171

'He goes with all of us. He is always available to all of us. Some of us know him, others do not.

'Those who recognise and follow him and those who hear his words — they are very blessed.'

'But he is not speaking now,' I objected.

'You are wrong, my son. He is speaking, but with words of silence that are only heard in our hearts. He is also speaking through those in a position of responsibility in his community, the Church. And he has also spoken in the past in human words, spoken, heard and meditated by his first companions assembled in their communities, and those words are recorded in the Book.

'If you really want to know what love is and how to love, you must read the Book and look at Jesus loving. In that Book, he has given us his great commandment: Love one another as I have loved you.'

'How do the Church leaders speak, then?' I asked.

'Jesus believed it was necessary to have leaders of the community and promised to help them with his Spirit. They interpret not only his words but also life itself. And they are able to say: You must do this or that if you are to love in this or that situation. Or, if you do this or that, you are not loving as Jesus wants you to love.'

'Not loving is, according to the Church leaders, sinning,' I said.

'Yes, that is right. Sinning is always loving badly or not loving at all. Jesus has, after all, given us only one commandment that sums up all the others — the commandment to love God and all our neighbours.'

'But there are certain kinds of love that are forbidden,' I exclaimed.

'No, there are none.'

'I do not remember the exact words, but surely Jesus said that desiring another man's wife was sinful.'

'Desiring her and wanting to take her as one's property, yes that is sinful, but it is not love!' the Sage said at once and went on: 'Just desiring a woman because she is desirable is not really sinful. But we have to purify our desires and even fight hard not to take what is not ours or not even offered to us. We also have to fight ourselves if we are to avoid taking from another person what he or she cannot give us. Those

172

struggles are a test of our love and, even though our weakness may make us fall, we should never cease struggling.

'Some people are able to live more fully from love on forbidden ways than others can on permitted ways. Everything depends on our heart! If we listen to our heart, we shall hear the voice of God speaking with words of silence.

'Jesus once told some men who scrupulously observed the rules and the laws that prostitutes would enter the kingdom of God before them. The way of love is clearly marked out, but sometimes the body takes a path that the heart does not want to follow. Only those who are alive know what is living in their hearts and only God can measure the force of love that makes those hearts beat.'

I think I understood what the Sage had been saying. Those in a position of responsibility in the Church, and who knew the way of love, had the task of teaching others. But they also had to listen to those who were on that way. Talking about love was, after all, one thing, but experiencing it in one's life was quite different.

As I got up to leave the Sage, I could not help saying: 'If those churchmen, who are, after all, not married, listened more to those who are, they might not speak in quite the same way about love.'

'That is what I think too,' the Sage observed. 'At least, they might say the same things, but differently and more encouragingly. They point to the end of the way, but we are on that way and our experience of it is sometimes very painful.

'I am convinced that the Spirit of Jesus is with them and that they have to speak, but I am equally convinced that the same Spirit is also with very many of those who are experiencing love and are trying to live as a couple in the light of the Word of God. They have a vital contribution to make. Reading the Word of God in the Gospel without listening to what God has to say to us in our lives is not complete in itself.'

Although I had been with him for a long time and he was obviously still unwell and tired, he had not quite finished.

'There are two conditions, each one with many variations, in which those who know with their heads but not with their bodies or hearts should either be silent or, if they speak, must do so with sensitivity and compassion. They are the con-

173

dition of suffering and that of love when either reaches such a point that we can call it "passion".

'You are, for example, with a sick person who is unable to pray or do anything but endure pain. How is it possible in that situation to utter fine words and say that his suffering is necessary?

'Or if you have never experienced the warmth of bodies tenderly entwined and the beating of two hearts at one with each other, how can you proclaim the rules and laws, however rational they may be, in the hope that they will put out the fire that is consuming the body and heart of the person in whose presence you are?

'At the foot of the cross, Mary said nothing. And in the presence of the woman taken in adultery, Jesus was silent. But I think they must have prayed.'

I thought, as I was going out, that the Sage must have suffered a great deal himself from fine words spread over his open wounds.

36

I had discovered another aspect of the Sage's personality. I already knew that he could be quite hard, even obstinate in his defence of the purity of love. Now, however, since our last encounter, he had shown me how wonderfully sensitive he could be to the difficulties encountered by lovers. This insight gave me strength. Loving, I now felt, was trying to love throughout the whole of one's life and saying again and again that unique word 'yes'.

I did not always understand at once what my Friend was saying. I sometimes just heard his words and reflected about them later. Very often, however, I grasped his meaning immediately. It seemed to go straight into my heart without touching my mind. At such times, my reaction was: I have known that for a long time!

What was it that he had said the last time I was with him? 'Sometimes the body takes a path that the heart does not want to follow.' I had understood that! It has been meant for me! I was, I knew, not yet completely in control of my body.

For a long time it had troubled me. When I was very young, like most children, I had discovered my body, explored it and, yes, loved it. But unfortunately, I had not been told that it was a friend, but had been put on my guard against it. That had made it difficult for me to get on happily with it!

Later on, I so much wanted my body to be strong and muscular and I suffered a great deal because it was not and because I did less well in games and physical combat than others of my own age.

Then, as I became older, I envied friends who were, I thought, better looking and so more attractive to girls than I was. Although I revealed it to no one, I felt handicapped and had to employ all kinds of ruses to make girls notice me. I found that humiliating.

I soon learned, however, that, even though my own body often embarrassed me and often made me suffer, it was also able to give me great pleasure. They were marvellous, but very fleeting, those moments of pleasure. They passed so quickly that I had to look for them again and again. But the more often I repeated them, the more insistently my longings returned and the more tyrannical they became.

Meeting girls became an obsession for me. I longed for the pleasure that they could give me and the need to satisfy that desire became my main reason for living. My friends shared those longings and went in search of the same adventures. We used to talk endlessly about it and our stories were bawdy. That was our experience of 'love'!

Since I had begun visiting the Sage, however, my attitude had gradually changed. I had become troubled in a way that I could not define, uneasy and often vaguely disgusted with myself. I was aware that I had made something very beautiful unclean. Despite all my efforts to look at girls in quite a different way, I was still often driven to take what I no longer really wanted to take . . .

I had for a long time now wanted to speak to the Sage about this inner struggle, but I had hardly dared to broach the subject. Now at last, however, I felt that I could. His tender words seemed to invite me to speak.

'Yes', the human body is beautiful,' my friend said at once. 'And a woman's body is especially beautiful. It is the man's way of looking at it that makes it unclean.

'A dirty hand takes away the freshness of the object that it wants to hold. You have to cleanse your eyes before you let them rest on a body. With clean eyes, a man can look, admire and respect . . .'

'My body is no longer beautiful and my face is only very commonplace,' I said.

'But true beauty is to be found in the clearness of the heart. Even the most beautiful lamp looks dull when its light is put out,' the Sage said. 'You will be beautiful when your heart begins to shine and your body becomes your heart's faithful and loving partner.'

'But my body is not faithful. I have let it run wild!'

Many men lead very fragmented lives. They say to their

176

bodies: You are quite free, do what you like! But none of us can develop properly if our spirit, our heart and our body are not living in unity. Man is one! God wanted us to be one and we cannot divide what God has united without grave risk to ourselves.

'What can you give of yourself, my son, if your body is not completely you? And what kind of life can you offer the other person, if you only offer an uninhabited body?

'Go and live in it again and say this to it:

'My body, you were my father's seed sown in the soil of
                                    my mother's body.
You were fashioned out of blood, flesh, smiles, songs
    and yes, perhaps also tears.
You were shaped to the rhythm of a beating heart,
    looking forward to the light of day.
You were given to me, my body, in unity with
    and at the same time as my heart and my spirit,
    so that not one part could say "I am"
    without being something other than me.
You were brought into the world, my body,
    to work on a very difficult site
    with other workmen who were committed to this earth
    and together with them you may build the kingdom.
You were bathed in water, my body,
    when, knowing that their child was also a child of God,
        your parents presented you to the Church of Jesus
                                            Christ
        so that you could become a living member of his Body.
You learned to speak, going much further than mere
                                            words,
        so that with your fingers, your lips and all that is in you
        you could enter into communion with another's body
        and say 'I love you' in the depth of an embrace
    and the two of you give a new brother or sister to men
    and a new son or daughter to God.

You were sent, my body, so that you might whisper
    to everyone, but especially to the one you love
    something about God.
                        177

For you should know, my body —
    when God wanted to come close to us
    and speak to us about his Love,
he asked the young woman Mary for a body
    and she made that body
    and gave it to him
    when she gave it to the world
    and he gave it to us
    and together and for ever
    we became one
    as he is one
    with his Father and his Spirit.'

The Sage looked at me for a moment, said: 'Say this to your
body as well,' and went on:

'My body, I do not want to treat you, who are wedded
                                                to my heart,
    just as an object of pleasure.
I do not want to use you like a tool
    that is picked up and thrown down
I do not want you to turn away from me
    like a deserter running from battle.
I do not want you, my body, to be separate from me —
    like my clothes, a disguise,
    something that betrays or hides me.
I do not want you to be always in flight,
    wandering far from home in search of pleasure,
    gathering fruit that I have not chosen.
I do not want you to lie about me, my body,
    whenever you speak about me.
I want to tune you in to my music
    so that your song will be true.
I want to question you every day
    so that your words will be true.

What do you say, my body,
    that may reveal my soul?

178

What do you say, my hand,
   clasping the hand of my friend?
What do you say, my look,
   that light of my heart in the window of my eyes?
What do you say, my smile,
   that open flower in the garden of my lips?
What do you say, my kiss,
   that breath of my life on the face of my loved one?

What will you say, my loving arms,
   that cradle my love with tenderness,
   when together we become one flesh?

What will you say, my weary limbs,
   when you are stricken with sickness
   and suffering from pain and loneliness?
And when my mouth is silent,
   will you, my eyes, still speak?
And when my eyes have closed
   and my face is cold,
will you, my love, still reflect
the light of my departed soul?

O my body given and loved,
   word of my soul,
   song of my love,
O my body, so often faithless,
   so often rebellious,
I want with all my strength
   to live in and with you!
Without you, I cannot be myself
   and without me you are just adrift
   and waiting to be wrecked.

Come back to me, my body!
We shall love together and give life
And our Lord Jesus Christ will take us together
   to the end of the road,
   beyond the grave
   to the resurrection.'

I was about to leave the Sage when the nurse came into the room. We could not avoid meeting and passing each other. She had the Child with her and he was obviously happy.

'You must not tire him,' she said to the Child. 'Just kiss him and say good-bye.'

She put her hand on the Sage's brow.

'You are feverish. You have been talking too much,' she said gently, almost affectionately. Then she turned to me and her voice became very firm: 'You should not have stayed so long!'

I left at once, thinking: 'I do not like that nurse very much!'

37

I had a woman friend who was much older than I was and who had not married. I had known her for a long time and I and my friends all called her 'serious', in other words, she was too serious for us. We always spoke about the girls we knew in categories, each with its own descriptive adjective. But most of us had a great respect for this 'serious' girl and I regarded her as an older sister, although I hardly dared to call her that or to let my friends know that I saw her in that light. I often used to talk to her, especially before I had met the Sage, and she had said things to me that the Sage had told me later. Sometimes I had found myself smiling afterwards about her ideas, thinking that they were no more than the dreams of a girl whose knowledge of love had come from books. I was different, of course. I knew from experience!

All the same, she interested me.

Then she moved away and I felt deprived of her friendship. Yes, I missed her and, now that I had come to know the Sage, I wished that I could still see her. I would, I know, have understood her much better.

Then, one day, I happened to meet her again. She was alone as usual. I was very happy to see her. She was, as always, smiling, but she was still serious and reserved. But there was, I felt quite sure now, a depth within her of which very few people would be aware. How foolish those young men had been to have walked at her side without even noticing her! If she had been a bit younger, I might have learned to love her!

We looked at each other for a long time. Then she spoke.

'You have changed!'

'How can you tell?'

'From your face. And even more from the way you are looking at me.'

'Yes, I have changed. I will tell you about it later.'

Was she hoping to meet someone? Or had she given up hope? Was she unhappy? I did not know. She said nothing about herself. She just smiled. Then, after a while, when we had arranged to see each other again, she went off.

I was sad for her and thought: It is not fair.

I decided to talk to the Sage about her.

He was quite seriously ill. He was lying on his bed wrapped in a heavy great-coat. He seemed smaller, thinner and older. But there was the same intensity in his eyes and the same warmth in his smile.

He made a great effort to get up and, despite my protestations, struggled into his armchair.

'We shall not have much time to talk today. My nurse will be back soon. She will not let you stay here with me! She is very strict and I have to obey her, you know!'

After I had told him about the young woman I had just met, he said:

'There are so many women who are hoping that a man will come along one day and say: "I love you," but whose hope is not fulfilled. Some of them are very unhappy.'

'Why do they meet no one, then? Is it God's will?'

'It is God's will that *everyone should love*,' he said emphatically. 'As for the rest, there is a mystery hidden in everyone's life. A mystery composed of the fruits of our freedom and others' freedom, of the events in our lives and of that nature that makes the rain fall and the sun shine because that is how it is.'

'But I remember being told that God directs our lives.'

'Someone else must have told you that — I did not! We direct our own lives — in the maze of our own and other people's decisions, most of which are indecipherable. And again and again we ask why, why, why — but hardly ever receive an answer. It is only much later, when we are in the Light, that we shall discover the meaning of each "yes" and each "no" in our lives and know how much love — or sin — each one contains.'

'I cannot understand what you are saying,' I told the Sage. 'You have spoken about God so often. Is he absent from our lives, then?'

182

'No, he is infinitely present, my son! Perhaps you have misunderstood me. God is a loving father. He goes along with each of his children, step by step. He is always at our side, but he lets us walk on our own. He offers us the Light and the Strength of his Love, so that we can live and walk with him and experience *what we have decided to experience in our lives.*'

'And what we have not decided to experience, but what is imposed on our lives — loneliness, for example? What about that?'

'If the situation exists and cannot be changed, then we have to *decide* sooner or later not just to endure it, but to experience it. Every event can be "providential" if we open ourselves to Love and find the strength *to want deeply to experience what we did not originally want.*'

'Is that how you would speak to a young woman who came to you to give her light on her lonely way? To that nice, virtuous young woman I have just told you about?'

'I would tell her first to look for a companion,' the Sage said.

'And then?'

'Then it would be her turn to speak, because she would have to decide.

'Hope . . .

My woman's heart beating with tenderness,
   my heart is available — an open flower
   blooming at every season of life!
Who will come and pick it from where it is growing?
Come soon, unknown one!
Some of the flowers I have offered
   have been thrown aside.
I have kept the rest of them,
   but they are fading.

My body, an island on whose soil
   no traveller has ever set foot!
On summer evenings I long to launch my boat
   and set sail in search of some explorer
   and bring him back to my shores.

183

He would seek and discover my hidden treasures!
And if he did not marry me for my gold and silver,
   it would at least have shone for him for a night.

But he did not come
   and I did not set sail on the sea.

The field of my body is waiting in vain
   for the seed of love —
and my arms for the children of my dreams!
What use is the soil if it bears no crop?
   And the tree's branches stretched out
   if they bear no fruit?
What use is my life, Lord,
   if I cannot give it to another?

I used to look at the boys who passed by
   and was quite untroubled.
I saw my friends look at them,
   stretch out their arms and take them.
Then I saw them come out of the church arm in arm.
And I was happy and smiled because they were happy.

But one after another they went on their way,
   at first in couples, then joined by a third,
   smiling or crying for milk,
and I was left alone at home, chosen by no one.

I have been told . . .

   Nice virtuous girl at the window, you see no one coming.
Do you perhaps hide when you hear the sound of boys'
                                 voices
   outside the window?
Have you perhaps grown up too quickly,
   so that the passer-by cannot meet your eyes
   when you gaze at the distant horizon?
Have you perhaps grown older too quickly,
   accepting too much work and responsibility,
   forgetting the rapid passage of the years?

Have you perhaps such a perfect image of love
   that the boy you encounter
   can only provide a rough sketch of it
   and you are disappointed with him?

   Nice virtuous girl at the window, you see no one coming.
Do not hope to hear a boy serenading under your balcony!
   In the past girls used to expect boys to make that music,
      but now you have to pluck the strings and sing as well.

Do not expect a boy to knock eagerly at your door!
   It was the boy who knocked and the girl who opened
                                                 the door,
      so it was said, at least, in the past.
But who said that and who had the right to say it?
   Surely your heart beats as strongly as a boy's!
What no one, neither boy nor girl, has the right to do
   is to force the door open when it is shut.

   Nice virtuous girl at the window, you see no one coming.
You must go down into the street — but not the deserted
                                                 street —
   and join in the dance of the young people
   who are looking for each other
and if you meet a boy you like — why wait?
   Just tell him you like him!
He too may perhaps not be able to imagine
   that one day he may find his way to a loving heart
                                            through a kiss.

If you feel no more than friendship and respect for him,
   go along with him and look for his heart and yours.
One day perhaps a silent string may sound in you
   and the face you thought plain may become attractive!
A look can, after all, light a fire that was waiting to be lit
   by someone putting a flame to it.

   Nice virtuous girl at the window, you see no one coming.
Do not, for heaven's sake, say that God is directing your
                                                 life
   and that you must wait for his decisions.

God is not the director of a marriage agency
   and the saints are not his staff, paid by a prayer.
He is our father and he loves his children
   and fathers do not love their children
   when they arrange their marriages in advance without
                                                    them.
But if you have looked patiently and for a long time
   and still have not found the companion you were
                                              seeking,
   do not give up hope!
No one can live a full life if he gives up hope!
And the single life is not a failed life,
   but a different way of life!
One day you will have to make a free decision
   and choose what you have so far not chosen.
Then you will want your 'yes' to be as free
   as the 'yes' that two lovers give each other.

I will rouse myself

and I too will marry . . .

Good-bye to my foolish dreams of passing love affairs,
   to false promises and to fickle and often imaginary lovers
   coming and going, haunting me day and night,
   slipping into my bed, making me restless
   and leaving me at dawn with nothing.

I have decided to divorce you, my dream, my fickle lover!
   I want to be free of you — free to love.

I have come a long way in my life,
   along straight roads and winding paths.
My heart has led me and guided my footsteps
   and now I have reached the first real turning-point.

I have stopped at the side of the road,
   reflecting, praying, weeping maybe,
   but I have agreed to look steadily ahead
   towards a way that is unknown,
   through the countryside of my future life.

186

I have glimpsed the road ahead, the road I have chosen.
My map shows only the ways of my longings
   and this road in front of me, my road, is unmapped,
   but I know it is the only one for me to take.
It will lead me, if I follow it faithfully,
   to many encounters that have been written on my
                                     itinerary,
   without my knowing, by countless events.

I shall respond to this call to go forward,
   this strange vocation I have so often rejected,
and make myself available at last
   and be open to whatever may happen —
   the unpredictable future that I am not seeking.
I shall go forward to the altar
   where my Lord is waiting for me
   and resolutely proclaim the 'yes' of my wedding
   at the end of such a long betrothal.

Yes, I would like you all to come to that wedding,
   but you will not see my partner —
   he has a thousand faces.
But I shall recognise him as he comes towards me
   with dragging steps and heart exhausted,
   looking for the bread of friendship and life given.
For a long time I thought I had to marry sad loneliness,
   but now I reject that fate and I marry many.

I shall be a drop of cool water on the faces
   of those who have never known the dew of tenderness.
I shall be arms opened wide to the child
   who is looking for a haven of affection.
I shall be yeast in the dough of mankind.
I shall plough waste land and sow seed
   where no one would ever spend time or money.
My heart is a great bag full of seed to be scattered!

With the sand of my life I shall mix the cement of love
   and I shall join those who build cities
   and work for justice and peace.

With them I shall build houses and temples
    for the children of the world.
And because no one is waiting for me in my bed,
    I shall stay awake while others rest
    So as to enter into communion with him.

I shall remain in your presence, Lord,
    with my heart wide open,
    repeating every day that "yes"
    repeated by faithful husbands and wives.
And you will tell me that you love me, as you love them,
    and that I must love, as they too have to love.

So with you I give up my life — I give life!
I shall be the mother of countless children,
    who will later come and welcome me, telling me their
                                 names,
    in the Light of your Father — the Father of the Living.

But I am a woman, Lord, and I shall always suffer
    from not knowing a man.
You understand me, Lord,
because you are a man and you have suffered
    from not having known a woman
    and from keeping your heart and your body available
    to give them in communion to all who are hungry.

When I come to the cross that I shall have to ascend,
    I shall not be alone and forsaken.
I have known for a long time that you have gone before me.
I shall join you, Lord, on that cross
    and together we shall come down from it.
Thanks to you, the cross is no longer a death-bed,
    but a way to a life.

And my life will be joy — today and in eternity.'

The Sage added a few words — very quickly and with his
eyes on the door. He was obviously expecting his nurse to
come in and find us still talking.

There was a knock at the door and she greeted us very

pleasantly, but I did not dare to look at her. I felt a bit guilty! The Sage gave me a knowing look. He was like a naughty little boy, amused by our disobedience!

The nurse went into the next room and her back was turned towards us. She must have been preparing the Sage's medicine. He beckoned me to come closer and whispered: 'She is nice, isn't she?'

His words completely took me aback. I felt myself blushing and whatever he might have wanted me to reply, all I could say, very sheepishly, was: 'Not bad!' — one of the categories I and my friends had used in the past.

I left as quickly as I could, but, outside, my first thought was: 'Yes, she is nice,' and I felt sorry I had not said so and happy that she was.

38

A few days later I found a note from the nurse in my letter-box. She had obviously written it in a hurry. There was no address, date or 'Dear . . .', but it was not difficult to know why. How would I have written to her? No differently! But I was still strangely disappointed that there was nothing in her letter that was at all friendly.

'Your friend is very tired,' I read. 'He has to go away and rest completely if he is to benefit from the care I can give him. He may be away for a long time. He has said he would like to see you before he goes. Will you come at the usual time tomorrow? But if you come, please do not tire him with your questions. You value his friendship, so think of him. His health gives cause for concern.'

So the Sage was seriously ill and had to go away. Would I ever see him again? I feared the worst and felt anxious and miserable. But at the same time, I was irritated by the nurse's letter. She seemed to know about my conversations with the Sage. Had he perhaps spoken to her about me? I doubted it, because I knew he was very discreet. Had she perhaps questioned him about me? She might be 'nice', but I did not like the way she told me off.

I decided to visit my friend earlier than our usual time in order to avoid her.

The Sage was half sitting up in bed, with a couple of pillows under his shoulders. He had difficulty in breathing. He brightened up as soom as I came in and signed to me to lift him in the bed, but I shook my head. He did not press me and I could see that weakness was the main reason for his compliance.

I did not ask him about his health. It was such a stereo-typed question, I felt, and I knew too that he would only reassure me, saying that he was getting on well.

I waited for him to say something, but he did what he always did — he waited for my questions. And I had plenty of important ones! But I had decided that he should give me only brief replies. I went to the heart of the matter at once.

'I have thought a great deal about what you told me when I was here last time,' I said, 'and now I know that a young person who has remained unmarried despite himself or herself should not just give up hope and be passively resigned to the single life, but should fully accept it. You cannot just live the whole of your life grudgingly. But what I do not understand is that some men and women can actually choose a celibate way of life. I think it is abnormal.'

'What is abnormal is not loving. Every man and woman is called to love, to marry and to give his or her life. That is everyone's vocation. But there are different ways of responding to that voication. Those who choose celibacy choose it out of love.

'What you are saying, then, is that, if priests do not marry, that is out of love — for God?'

'*Out of love for Jesus Christ and his Church*, the people of God, the men, women and children gathered together by him.

'The bishops are the successors of the Apostles and they ask some Christians to agree to leave everything in order to follow Jesus Christ and serve his Church. Those men will work with their bishops and proclaim the Gospel to everyone, gather the community of believers around Christ and make them one Body through the Eucharist.'

'But surely they could dedicate themselves to that task just as well if they were married!'

'It might be possible for them to do it with difficulty, but they could do it, certainly. But for many centuries now, the Church has insisted that the priest should dedicate his body, his heart, his spirit and the whole of his life to that task.'

'But why?'

'In imitation of Jesus and out of love for him who has given himself without any reservation to his "people", making a covenant with them. He is "married" to them and has offered them not only his heart, which is always available to them, but also his body, which is entirely "reserved" for them. He will continue to give his body to them in communion until the end of time.'

'But surely Jesus never himself required priests to make a gift of themselves like that?'

'No, he did not. Not explicitly. But love does not "require". It offers itself. The Church may one day decide to act differently.'

'Would you like that to happen?'

'Yes, I would like that. But at the same time, I would also with all my strength like men voluntarily to go, out of love, to the very limit of their gift of themselves. Jesus after all said: "Greater love has no man than this, that a man lay down his life for his friends".'

'But priests do not always bear witness to a love like that!'

'They try to, I think, but do not always succeed.'

'Where are we to find that witness borne, then?'

'Some bear witness to that love from the summit of the mountain because they reach the summit. But others try again and again to reach it and never do. They bear witness to the value of devoting one's life to the attempt.'

The Sage paused and, when he resumed, he spoke in a very quiet voice. 'Married couples are also called to bear witness. In the sacrament of marriage, they commit themselves to the task of reflecting Jesus' faithful love of his Church.'

He paused again.

'But not every couple succeeds in bearing witness to that love.'

He said no more and I respected his sad silence.

I wondered whether I ought to continue with this conversation. I had the feeling that the nurse was looking at me. I knew she was not there, of course, but it was not easy to rid myself of the sense of her disapproving presence. But I still had questions to ask him!

'What you have been saying is this: priests have been called to an essential service in the Church and they have agreed, out of love, to leave everything in order to serve the Church in this way. But I still do not understand what purpose religious — monks and nuns — are serving.

'I can understand those who dedicate themselves to the service of the deprived and the underprivileged. I can understand those who go into the world to proclaim the Good News. But I cannot understand those who join enclosed

orders . . . I no longer think, as I used to, that they are
either mad or foolish. But I still wonder why they do that.
What is the secret in their life that makes them choose that
way — what is the mystery?'

I knew my Friend would reply to my question and I knew
I had a deep need of his reply. Not just to satisfy my intellec-
tual curiosity or to answer the sarcastic questions I feared my
friends would ask. No, I needed his reply in order to be able
to experience the life of love.

'Men and women —
    you cling to this earth, believing it is eternal,
    you eat too much because you think you are starving,
    you hold each other in your possessive arms.
Men — you want to tear happiness from the untamed
                                                universe,
    probe its secrets and control its forces.
    You build towers of concrete and steel,
    striving to reach up to the gates of heaven.
Men — you get up every morning and work and struggle,
    go back to bed in order to rise and struggle again
    and then, your work still undone, you die.
Men and women —
    you make children because you have to make them,
    children who will get up and work and struggle
    and go to bed in order to rise and struggle again
    and then, their work unfinished, die like their parents.

Men and women —
    hard-headed and unquestioning, do you understand?

What purpose does the flower serve
    if it is born and dies hidden among the weeds,
and the beautifully carved stone
    if it is at the summit of the cathedral spire?
or the star shining in the sky at night
    if it is only one among countless others?

What purpose does the musician serve
    playing alone behind a closed door?

193

or the picture that is worth a fortune
   if it is kept close-guarded and hidden from view?
or the young mother standing alone and motionless,
   gazing down in rapture at her sleeping baby?

What purpose does the blind man serve
   since he cannot see?
or the deaf person who cannot hear?
   or the lame man who cannot walk?
   or the old woman who is waiting to die?

What purpose does anyone serve
   who is there for no reason,
   alongside someone else who happens to be there?

Men and women — do you understand at all?

If you do not understand or no longer understand
   you must be the most wretched of people,
   because you will never know what purpose is served
                                             by living
   and you will never know what it is simply to love.

Lord, we need, yes, we urgently need
   to see in the midst of us men and women
   who seem to serve no purpose at all except to love.
Lord, we need to discover and believe
   that Love is everything —
   the life-force, breath, blood and life itself
   of this great humanity that we are.

Lord, look at us!
   We are only poor men and women,
   walking with our noses in the dust,
   our feet covered in mud,
   our hearts enmeshed in our little cares and joys
   and our spirits raised by our wonderful achievements.

Lord, send us men and women filled with Love —
   not to be our models, as we have many of those,
   not to distract us from our tasks
   and not to overshadow our own loves,

but just to be among us as visible signs
and as light in the darkness of our lives,
bearing witness to what is essential.

The purpose that they will serve will be to remind us
that our world is beautiful, but that in it
another Kingdom is growing mysteriously —
a Kingdom that will never end,
and that happiness is to be found
not just in the things of this earth,
but in the Word that is heard
and experienced in faith and trust.

And they will also show us
that the greatest freedom is not to be found
in doing what we want to do,
but often in freely yielding in love.

They may also be able to prove in their lives
that the language of love is not just language of bodies.
Bodies will after all cease to speak one day,
while hearts will continue to sing.

And they will also prove
that life can be given in ways
that are not those of the flesh
and that the whole of life can be fruitful
if it is filled and inspired with love.

Happy are those who can see
those men and women whose hearts
are open to the joy and suffering of this world,
those communities of brothers and sisters
who watch and wait, let themselves be loved
and thank and praise the one they contemplate,
the one in whose invisible presence they live,
the one who is God and who is called Love.

Happy are those who are able to understand
that, if God is really God,

195

it is right that some should live
recollected in body, heart and mind
for him, their lives freely offered to him,
because his is there, and freely offered for us.'

I could see that the Sage was praying now. He was silent
for a long time, then he said:
'My dear boy, what would we do in the future if there
were no more of those men and women among us who
respond to the invitation of the Spirit and becomes signs
for us — signs of that love that goes infinitely beyond love
and is above all free?'
He said no more and sank into a deep silence.
I felt peaceful and very happy. At last I had understood.
And for the first time I discovered that I was no longer
afraid. I still felt very weak, but I knew that I was at last
ready to try to love.
The Sage was clearly very tired. He had spoken passion-
ately and often very forcefully. I was very sorry that I had
been so eager to hear his response to my questions that I
had exhausted him. But I had been so thirsty for his words!
I felt this might be the last time that I would be able to
quench my thirst at this spring.
I heard footsteps outside. The nurse would be in the room
in another moment! I felt suddenly uneasy and anxious, like
a child caught playing a forbidden game.
The Sage knew what was troubling me. He smiled and said:
'What does it matter? It will be the last time.' He sighed.
'A pity — because there is still so much to be said.'
She came in. She seemed to shine like a ray of sunlight
and, when she spoke, she seemed to be singing. I had not
noticed before that her voice sang!
'How are you today? Still tired?'
'I am getting on very well. We have been talking, my friend
and I.'
'I can see that.' She looked at me, but this time there was
no sign of reproach in her eyes. Then very quickly, as though
she wanted to shake off a vague anxiety, she added: 'You
have no bad feelings towards me, I hope?'

Bad feelings about what?'

'About the letter I wrote to you. I was not sure how to express myself. We hardly knew each other . . .'

I thought she sounded sorry and that pleased me. I too felt sorry that her letter had disappointed me.

'Think no more of it! I would have written in much the same way in your position.'

She smiled. I thought: She is really much nicer than I had believed!

I wanted to go on talking to her, but she had turned to the Sage.

'I have to get your medicines ready for the night. I will come back at about ten o'clock and stay with you. I will sit in that chair. I will give you everything the doctor has prescribed and at the right times. Don't worry! I may fall asleep, but I will wake up.'

So she was going to stay up all night with him. I thought suddenly: But why should I not stay up with him? Surely my place was beside my friend?

I told her and she said nothing, but just looked enquiringly at the Sage. He nodded gently and, to my great surprise, she said at once:

'Of course you should stay and I will come back in the morning to give him an injection. I will show you all the medicines he needs to take during the night. When I have given him his morning injection, he will go away. I will come very early in the morning, because he has a long journey.'

I felt a deep sadness, but at the same time I was glad to be able to spend this last night with my friend. And I knew that he was very glad too. I thanked the nurse and she returned my thanks. We had, I knew, become friends.

39

I got up from the armchair in which I had been sitting and went closer to the Sage's bed. He was asleep. I stood contemplating his face for a long time, tracing the furrows on his brow. I seemed to hear his heart singing. His face, old and beautiful, was silent but singing and I listened to the music that it was making for me.

I was glad to stay up with him, watching.

Then I thought of the men and women we had been speaking about. The Sage had called them brothers and sisters who watch and wait. They were hearts beating in God's presence, awake and watching while others slept. They were there, living for God, because he is there. They were love. And I was there too now, living for one night at least for my friend, freely offering my life for a little time to him. Yes, I loved him. I wanted to tell him that, but he was asleep.

I was at one with all those who watch and wait. I had entered the great stream of love and life that flows through the world and I was still astonished that it was possible to love like that — to love without a word or a movement, without anyone knowing. In the night.

I prayed.

I did what the nurse had instructed me to do. It was not difficult. She had left the Sage's drugs in order and I could hardly make a mistake.

How old was she? She had been a nurse for two years, the Sage had told me once and that, with her training, would make her, I imagined, a little younger than me.

But she seemed very young! Perhaps her hair style made her look young. And her eyes! They shone with the clear cool light of spring. How could I ever have been irritated by her?

I touched the Sage's hand lightly and he opened his eyes.
'It is time for your medicine.'
He drank, then put his head back on the pillow. I thought
he had fallen asleep again, but no, he was looking at me.
'I have something more to tell you.'
'You must sleep.'
'We have so little time . . .'
'We have spoken enough already!'
'But only about certain aspects of the love that gives life
to everyone in this world!

'No one's heart will grow
    unless his head, his arms and his feet grow
    and no one will grow to maturity
    unless his brothers and sisters grow with him.
Mankind can only develop together with the universe,
    as matter and life have to be controlled and ordered.
History will not move forward
    unless we freely recognise the one walking with us,
    setting us free from what prevents us from loving
    and offering us his Life so that we may love with him.

'*Everyone is there, but there is only one way, and it goes
from Love to Love, with the one who is Love.*' The Sage
smiled. 'And each one of us has to be there. Loving.'
'There,' I repeated, 'But where is that?'
'I used to ask myself that question again and again:
    Where is that "there"?
People were waiting for me — people on the way.
    and each one of them was there —
        there in his own place.
And I was looking for my place,
    again and again thinking how useless I was.
Then I found that place, that "there",
    at my feet, just where I was.

You will find that "there", just where you are.
    Look!
God always gives us a sign
    in the events of our lives.'

199

'When you come back we will talk again,' I said.
But he did not reply.

God always gives us a sign in the events of our lives. The
Sage was right. God had given me a clear sign and had spoken
to me in this strange and wonderful encounter with the Sage.

But was what had happened to me really so extraordinary?
Is it not every living person's destiny to meet brothers and
sisters who will be 'word' for him and to experience events
that will be 'signs'. Each of us had to look and listen and let
that Word that is in the 'word' and that Light that enables
him to see be born and grow in his heart.

I knew with enormous sadness that I was with my Friend
for the last time and that I would probably never see him
again. But at the same time I also knew I would continue to
hear his voice, because it was another Voice that I heard
when I was listening to his voice. And that Voice would never
be silent — so long as I was faithful.

I thought of the nurse. Had she too something to say to
me? Clearly she had. But we hardly knew one another. She
seemed to want to know me better . . . I had not really looked
at her or listened to her.

Why had I again and again turned away from that look
that invites the other person to go out of himself? What
would her heart have said, for example, as I listened to her
words? I felt very sorry that I had been so inattentive.

'What are you thinking about?' the Sage asked me suddenly.

I was startled, because I had thought he was asleep. But he
had been watching me attentively.

'She is nice, isn't she?' he said.

This time I said 'yes'.

He closed his eyes and smiled.

'She is more than "nice",' he added. 'She has a good heart.
And so have you.'

I knew that he would say no more now.

When dawn broke I was very drowsy and my mind was at
rest, for I had done exactly what the nurse had told me to do.

The Sage was already awake.

'There is something more that I have to say. I think I have
not sufficiently stressed that love is Joy. God wants it to be

200

a joyful experience. When two people meet and their hearts are united and their bodies and the whole of their lives are one, a great happiness is born in them. If their love is true, that flame of happiness can never be extinguished.

'True love is entering the infinite Joy of God.

'I have met so many young people who think love is easy and then later I have found them heart-broken or angry because their dream has been shattered. I have wanted to impress on you not only how beautiful, but also how difficult love is. I have told you about my own experience! For me love was often suffering.'

'Did I make you suffer when I asked you to speak to me about love?' I asked. 'I am sorry if I did.'

'I am not sorry that I have loved,' the Sage said.

'You have suffered — but you have loved.'

'I have not loved enough. We can never love enough!'

'Are you troubled?'

'No, I am happy and at peace, because I know I am loved by the one who is Love.'

It would not be long now before I had to say good-bye to the Sage. I would not see him again. I knew that. We would not talk together again. I would go to the Source of his understanding of Love — the 'Book' — but I needed a face to love and a hand to rest lovingly on mine. I needed the tangible presence of a fellow human being to know that I was loved.

And how much I wanted my Friend to know who was going to share my life. He had, after all, written to me about 'my beautiful love as yet unknown'!

A question that I knew I had to ask him rose up from deep within me and I had to hear his reply.

'God does not choose the one with whom I will share my life, but does he know in advance the one I will choose?'

'God is Father. He sees all his children. Why, then, should he not want this man and that woman to meet and know each other? Many fathers here on earth, loving fathers, want this to happen, but they can make mistakes. God the Father does not make mistakes because his love is perfect. He knows where his children's happiness lies and sometimes he gives a discreet sign in the events of our lives or in the people we meet. But we are human and he leaves us free. If his children are faithful and watchful, what they want will coincide with what he wants. And when that happens, joy will break out — their joy in his Joy.'

I had carried out all the nurse's instructions and my friend seemed to be sleeping. The sun was rising now and it was going to be a bright, clear day. This would be my last hour with him. Why did it seem so long? Was I tired because of lack of sleep? No, I felt wide awake and very happy, even though I was about to be separated from my friend. And I was impatient. I was waiting, looking forward. But to what?

In a flash I knew. I was waiting for her! She had said she would be back 'very early in the morning'. The thought that I had held back for so long burst out, bringing with it an intense joy that I did not at first recognise, because I had never experienced it before. I was strongly tempted to waken the Sage and tell him, but now he was certainly asleep.

Ahead of me was a long journey of discovery. I had so much to discover about her! I had so many questions to ask her, but I, who had always been so bold with girls, knew in my heart that I would be too nervous and shy to put them to her.

Then I heard her footsteps outside as I had heard them the previous evening. My heart began to beat faster. She came in, looked at the Sage and then at me, putting her finger to her lips. But he had already heard her too and said quietly: 'Is it time to go now?'

She smiled and nodded, then, turning to me, said: 'You must say good-bye to your Friend now. Then I will give him an injection and get him ready for the journey.'

He was looking at us — first at one, then at the other and back again. He was smiling and happy.

'It is beautiful,' he said. 'A new day has dawned.'

He took my hand.

'Leave us together for a moment, while she gets me ready. It will not take long.' He smiled mischievously and I knew he had heard my heart singing before I was conscious of it myself. 'Then come back for her. You must not let her walk home alone through the deserted streets.'

I looked at her. I was not too nervous or shy to do that, but I could not speak. She opened her mouth, then closed it again. She smiled and that smile contained the one word I needed: 'yes'.

When I came back into the room again, the Sage was ready, waiting peacefully on his bed. Beside him on the floor was a case — such a little case for such a long journey! He saw me looking at it.

'There is no need to take much luggage when you are setting off in life. All that you need is love.'

He looked at both of us for a long time with great affection.

Then he said, in a voice that showed clearly that he did not wish to linger over farewells: 'It is time to go now, my children.'

She bent over him and kissed him.

'Be happy,' he said.

I embraced him and said: 'Thank you, father. You have given me life.'

'Good-bye, my dear child.'

He smiled and there were tears in his eyes. We were crying too.

I could not move and I could not take my eyes off his face. Then she came closer to me and I felt her hand take mine.

She took me outside and we watched our Friend as he was taken out. His eyes were closed, but his lips were moving and we heard him say again: 'There is no need to take much luggage when you are setting off in life. All that you need is love.'

Outside in the street the sun was shining.

Index of Meditations

Index of Meditations

These meditations can be used outside their context.